DWELLINGS

DWELLINGS

*A Spiritual History
of the Living World*

LINDA HOGAN

W. W. Norton & Company
New York   London

Printed in the United States of America
First published as a Norton paperback 2007

Manufacturing by LSC Harrisonburg
Book design by Chris Welch
Production manager: Devon Zahn

Library of Congress Cataloging-in-Publication Data

Hogan, Linda
    Dwellings : a spiritual history of the living world / by Linda Hogan
       p. cm.
    1. Philosophy of nature. I. Title
    BD581.H573   1995
    113–dc20   95-1725

ISBN 0-393-03784-3 (hardcover)
ISBN 978-0-393-32247-7 pbk.

W. W. Norton & Company, Inc.
500 Fifth Avenue, New York, N.Y. 10110
www.wwnorton.com

W. W. Norton & Company Ltd.
15 Carlisle Street, London W1D 3BS

8 9 0

FOR MY GRANDMOTHERS,
AND FOR GRANDMOTHER,
THE GOLDEN EAGLE.

ACKNOWLEDGMENTS

Some of these pieces have appeared or are forthcoming in the following publications: "The Voyagers," in *Religion and Literature;* "Waking up the Rake," in *Parabola;* "The Snake People," in *Icarus;* "A Different Yield," in *Religion and Literature;* "The Bats," in *The American Voice;* "Porcupine," in *The American Voice;* "Creations," in *The Nature Conservancy, The Last Great Places Anthology;* "The Kill Hole," in *Parabola;* "Stories of Water," in *New Letters;* "Walking," in *Parabola;* "Dwellings," in *Indiana Review;* "Caves," in *Sierra;* "Feathers," in *New Age.*

CONTENTS

PREFACE

As an Indian woman I question our responsibilities to the caretaking of the future and to the other species who share our journeys. These writings have grown out of those questions, out of wondering what makes us human, out of a lifelong love for the living world and all its inhabitants. They have grown, too, out of my native understanding that there is a terrestrial intelligence that lies beyond our human knowing and grasping.

It has been my lifelong work to seek an understanding of the two views of the world, one as seen by native people and the other as seen by those who are new and young on this continent. It is clear that we have strayed from the treaties we once had with the land and with the animals. It is also clear, and heartening, that in our time there are many—Indian and non-Indian alike—who want to restore and honor these broken agreements.

This work not only is tempered by my work with animals, my love for earth, my hunger to know what dwells beneath the surface of things; it also stretches to reflect the different histories of ways of thinking and being in the world. These writings, too, search out a world of different knowings, enter a doorway into the mythical world, a reality known by my ancestors, one that takes the daily into dimensions both sacred and present.

People, animals, land—the alive and conscious world—populate *Dwellings* in this exploration of the human place within this world. I write out of respect for the natural world, recognizing that humankind is not separate from nature. Some of this work connects the small world of humans with the larger universe, containing us in the same way that native ceremonies do, showing us both our place and a way of seeing.

These are lessons learned from the land and it is my hope that this work contributes to an expanded vision of the world. *Dwellings* is both of and about this alive and conscious world. Its pages come from forests, its words spring from the giving earth.

DWELLINGS

THE FEATHERS

*"Our task is to enter into the dream of Nature and
interpret the symbols."*
    —E. L. Grant Watson, *The Mystery of Physical Life*

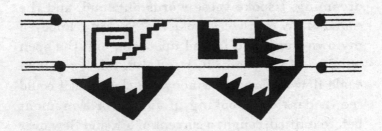

FOR YEARS I PRAYED FOR AN EAGLE FEATHER. I WANTED
one from a bird still living. A killed eagle would offer
me none of what I hoped for. A bird killed in the
name of human power is in truth a loss of power
from the world, not an addition to it.

My first eagle feather, one light and innocent, was
given to me by a traditional healer I'd gone to see
when I was sick. He told me a story about feathers.
When he was a child his home had burned down. All
that survived the fire were eagle feathers. They
remained in the smoking ruins of their home, floating on top of black ash and water. The feather he

gave me was one of those. I still keep it safe in a cedar box in my home.

Where I live is in a mountain canyon. It is not unusual to see golden eagles in the canyon, far above us. One morning, after all my years of praying for a feather, I dreamed I was inside a temple. It was a holy place. Other people were there, looking at the ornately decorated walls, the icons of gold, the dried and revered bodies of saints, but my attention was turned toward the ceiling. It was pink and domed, engraved with gold designs of leaves and branches. "Look up," I said to the others. "Look up." Still dreaming, I spoke these words out loud, and the sound of my own voice woke me. Waking, I obeyed my own words and looked up, seeing out the open window of my room. Just as I did, a large golden eagle flew toward the window, so close that I could see its dark eyes looking in at me for a moment before it lifted, caught a current of air, and flew over the roof of the house. I jumped up and ran barefoot outside to see where it was going.

If I told you the eagle was not in sight, and that there was a feather in the road when I reached it, you would probably not believe me. I, too, have seen how long it takes a feather to land, carried as they are by unseen currents of air. Once I waited for a hawk feather to fall. I covered distance, looking up, to follow it, but it never set down. It merely drifted until it was no longer in sight. But on the day of my dream, a feather was there. On the ground had fallen the gift of an eagle, soft white with a darker, rounded tip.

I know there is a physics to this, a natural law

about lightness and air. This event rubs the wrong way against logic. How do I explain the feather, the bird at my window, my own voice waking me, as if another person lived in me, wiser and more alert. I can only think there is another force at work, deeper than physics and what we know of wind, something that comes from a world where lightning and thunder, sun and rain clouds live. Nor can I say why it is so many of us have forgotten the mystery of nature and spirit, while for tens of thousands of years such things have happened and been spoken by our elders and our ancestors.

WHEN MY GRANDDAUGHTER, Vivian, entered her life in the world of air, I was at her emergence to greet her and to cut her cord, the sustaining link between her and her mother, her origins. When the bronze-colored stem of the baby dried, we placed it in a tall black pot until I could make and bead an umbilical bag to contain that first point of connection to this life, to keep her with us, safe and well.

One day a few months later, my parents visited. As always my father's presence turned us toward our identity and origins, so we brought out the cradle-board. My daughter, Tanya, dressed in her traditional beadwork clothing. Then, suddenly, with a look of horror, she said, "It's gone!" and ran toward the black jar that contained the baby's cord. She was right, the cord, the most valuable thing in our home, was no longer there. Because of the height and shape of the pot, and because of its placement on the shelves, it was not possible that wind might have carried it away. Nor could an animal have reached inside.

All that evening I searched, on hands and knees, under chairs, in corners, drawers, looking through the entire house, under furniture, on shelves, until no place was left unseen.

Several times throughout the night of searching, I opened a cedar box that contained tobacco, cornmeal, sage, and my first eagle feather, the one that lived through fire. Again and again I returned to the box, puzzled by my own behavior. Each time, as I opened it, I wondered why I was so compelled, so drawn to the container. It is a small box, with no hidden place where the birth cord might have been unnoticed, yet I returned to it. Opening it, looking inside, closing it.

In the middle of all this searching, a Blackfeet friend called to invite us to an encampment in Montana. "I'm so glad you called," I said to him. "I've lost my granddaughter's umbilical cord." I told him how terrible I felt about losing it and that perhaps the cord wanted to be elsewhere, maybe on the South Dakota reservation of my daughter's origins. Or that it was a sign to me that I have neglected my spiritual life, which I often do when working and living and teaching in a world of different knowings.

He told me a ceremony that might work. I hung up the phone and went to prepare the rite. Soon I was walking uphill in the dark, moonlit night toward a cluster of trees where I made the offering. Around me was the song of insects, a nighthawk with its high-pitched call and clattering wings.

When I returned, I went once again to the cedar box. This time the feather, something else of value to me, was gone. I didn't know how this could be. Yes, I opened the box several times, but the feather never moved.

Getting down on hands and knees I looked under a chair, and I saw the eagle feather there, and the feather was pointing at the umbilical cord, so mysteriously now on the floor I had already searched.

It was the feather that took me to the baby's umbilical cord. The feather, that element of bird, so formed, so groomed to catch the wind and lift, that one-time part of a whole flying. It had once seen distances, had risen and fallen beneath the sun.

PERHAPS THERE ARE events and things that work as a doorway into the mythical world, the world of first people, all the way back to the creation of the universe and the small quickenings of earth, the first stirrings of human beings at the beginning of time. Our elders believe this to be so, that it is possible to wind a way backward to the start of things, and in so doing find a form of sacred reason, different from ordinary reason, that is linked to forces of nature. In this kind of mind, like in the feather, is the power of sky and thunder and sun, and many have had alliances and partnerships with it, a way of thought older than measured time, less primitive than the rational present. Others have tried for centuries to understand the world by science and intellect but have not yet done so, not yet understood animals, finite earth, or even their own minds and behavior. The more they seek to learn the world, the closer they come to the spiritual, the magical origins of creation.

There is a still place, a gap between worlds, spoken by the tribal knowings of thousands of years. In it are silent flyings that stand aside from human struggles and the designs of our own makings. At times, when we are silent enough, still enough, we take a step into such mystery, the place of spirit, and mystery, we must remember, by its very nature does not wish to be known.

There is something alive in a feather. The power of it is perhaps in its dream of sky, currents of air, and the silence of its creation. It knows the insides of clouds. It carries our needs and desires, the stories of our brokenness. It rises and falls down elemental space, one part of the elaborate world of life where fish swim against gravity, where eels turn silver as moon to breed.

How did the feather arrive at the edge of the dirt road where I live? How did it fall across and through currents of air? How did the feathers survive fire? This I will never know. Nor will I know what voice spoke through my sleep. I know only that there are simple powers, strange and real.

THE BATS

THE FIRST TIME I WAS FORTUNATE ENOUGH TO CATCH A glimpse of mating bats was in the darkest corner of a zoo. I was held spellbound, seeing the fluid movement of the bats as they climbed each other softly and closed their wings together. They were an ink black world hanging from a rafter. The graceful angles of their dark wings opened and jutted out like an elbow or knee poking through a thin, dark sheet. A moment later it was a black, silky shawl pulled tight around them. Their turning was beautiful, a soundless motion of wind blowing great dark dunes into new configurations.

A few years later, in May, I was walking in a Minneapolis city park. The weather had been warm and humid. For days it had smelled of spring, but the morning grew into a sudden cold snap, the way Minnesota springs are struck to misery by a line of cold that travels in across the long, gray plains. The grass was crisp. It cracked beneath my feet. Chilled to the bone, and starting home, I noticed what looked like a brown piece of fur lying among the frosted blades of new grass. I walked toward it and saw the twiglike legs of a bat, wings folded like a black umbrella whose inner wires had been broken by a windstorm.

The bat was small and brown. It had the soft, furred body of a mouse with two lines of tiny black nipples exposed on the stomach. At first I thought it was dead, but as I reached toward it, it turned its dark, furrowed face to me and bared its sharp teeth. A fierce little mammal, it looked surprisingly like an angry human being. I jumped back. I would have pulled back even without the lightning fast memory of tales about rabid bats that tangle in a woman's hair.

In this park, I'd seen young boys shoot birds and turtles. Despite the bat's menacing face, my first thought was to protect it. Its fangs were still bared, warning me off. When I touched it lightly with a stick, it clamped down like it would never let go. I changed my mind; I decided it was the children who needed protection. Still, I didn't want to leave it lying alone and vulnerable in the wide spiny forest of grass blades that had turned sharp and brittle in the cold. Rummaging through the trash can I found a lidded box and headed back toward the bat when I came across another bat. This bat, too, was lying brown and inert on the grass. That's when it occurred to me that the recent warm spell had been broken open by the cold and the bats, shocked back into hibernation, had stopped dead in flight, rendered inactive by the quick drop in temperature.

I placed both bats inside the box and carried them home. Now and then the weight would shift and there was the sound of scratching and clawing. I wondered if the warmth from my hands was enough heat to touch them back to life.

At home, I opened the box. The two bats were mating. They were joined together, their broken umbrella wings partly open, then moving, slumping, and opening again. These are the most beautiful turnings, the way these bodies curve and glide together, fold and open. It's elegant beyond compare, more beautiful than eels circling each other in the dark waters.

I put them in a warm corner outside, nestled safe in dry leaves and straw. I looked at them several times a day. Their fur, in the springtime, was misted with dewy rain. They mated for three days in the moldering leaves and fertile earth, moving together in that liquid way, then apart, like reflections on a mirror, a four-chambered black heart beating inside the closed tissue of wings. Between their long, starry finger bones were dark webbings of flesh, wings for sailing jagged across the evening sky. The black wing membranes were etched like the open palm of a human hand, stretched open, offering up a fortune for the reading. As I watched, the male stretched out, opened his small handlike claws to scratch his stomach, closed them again, and hid the future from my eyes.

By the fourth day, the male had become thin and exhausted. On that day he died and the female flew away with the new life inside her body.

For months after that, the local boys who terrorized the backyards of neighbors would not come near where I lived. I'd shown one the skeleton of the male and told them there were others. I could hear them talking in the alley late at night, saying, "Don't go in there. She has bats in her yard." So they'd smoke their cigarettes in a neighbor's yard while the neighbor watched them like a hawk from her kitchen window. My house escaped being vandalized.

MY FAMILY LIVED in Germany once when I was a child. One day, exploring a forest with a friend, we came across a cave that went back into the earth. The dark air coming from inside the cave was cool, musty, and smelled damp as spring, but the entryway itself was dark and forboding, the entrance to a world we didn't know. Gathering our courage, we returned the next day with flashlights and stolen matches. It was late afternoon, almost dusk, when we arrived back at the cave. We had no more than just sneaked inside and held up the light when suddenly there was a roaring tumult of sound. Bats began to fly. We ran outside to twilight just as the sky above us turned gray with a fast-moving cloud of their ragged wings, flying up, down, whipping air, the whole sky seething. Afraid, we ran off toward the safety of our homes, half-screaming, half-laughing through the path in the forest. Not even our skirts catching on the brambles slowed us down.

Later, when we mentioned the cave of bats, we were told that the cave itself had been an ammunition depot during World War II, and that bat guano was once used in place of gunpowder. During the war, in fact, the American military had experimented with bats carrying bombs. It was thought that they could be used to fly over enemy lines carrying explosives that would destroy the enemy. Unfortunately, one of them flew into the attic of the general's house and the bomb exploded. Another blew up a colonel's car. They realized that they could not control the direction a bat would fly and gave up on their strategy of using life to destroy life.

Recently I visited a cave outside of San Antonio with writer and friend Naomi Nye. It was only a small mouth of earth, but once inside it, the sanctuaries stretched out for long distances, a labyrinth of passageways. No bats have inhabited that cave since people began to intrude, but it was still full of guano. Some of it had been taken out in the 1940s to be used as gunpowder. Aside from that, all this time later, the perfect climate inside the cave preserved the guano in its original form, with thick gray layers, as fresh and moist as when the bats had lived there.

Bats hear their way through the world. They hear the sounds that exist at the edges of our lives. Leaping through blue twilight they cry out a thin language, then listen for its echo to return. It is a dusky

world of songs a pitch above our own. For them, the
world throws back a language, the empty space rising between hills speaks an open secret then lets the
bats pass through, here or there, in the dark air.
Everything answers, the corner of a house, the shak-
ing leaves on a wind-blown tree, the solid voice of
bricks. A fence post talks back. An insect is located. A
wall sings out its presence. There are currents of air
loud as ocean waves, a music of trees, stones, charred
stovepipes. Even our noisy silences speak out in a
dark dimension of sound that is undetected by our
limited hearing in the loud, vibrant land in which we
live.

Once, Tennessee writer Jo Carson stuck her hearing aid in my ear and said, "Listen to this." I could
hear her speak, listening through the device. I could
hear the sound of air, even the noise of cloth moving
against our skin, and a place in the sky. All of it
drowned out the voices of conversation. It was how a
bat must hear the world, I thought, a world alive in
its whispering songs, the currents of air loud as waves
of an ocean, a place rich with the music of trees and
stones.

It is no wonder that bats have been a key element
in the medicine bundles of some southern tribes. Bats
are people from the land of souls, land where moon
dwells. They are listeners to our woes, hearers of
changes in earth, predictors of earthquake and storm.
They live with the goddess of night in the lusty
mouth of earth.

Some of the older bundles, mistakenly opened by
non-Indians, were found to contain the bones of a

bat, wrapped carefully in brain-tanned rawhide. The skeletons were intact and had been found naturally rather than killed or trapped by people, which would have rendered them neutral; they would have withdrawn their assistance from people. Many Indian people must have waited years, searching caves and floors and the ground beneath trees where insects cluster, in order to find a small bony skull, spine, and the long finger bones of the folded wings. If a bat skeleton were found with meat still on it, it was placed beside an anthill, and the ants would pick the bones clean.

I believe it is the world-place bats occupy that allows them to be of help to people, not just because they live inside the passageways between earth and sunlight, but because they live in double worlds of many kinds. They are two animals merged into one, a milk-producing rodent that bears live young, and a flying bird. They are creatures of the dusk, which is the time between times, people of the threshold, dwelling at the open mouth of inner earth like guardians at the womb of creation.

The bat people are said to live in the first circle of holiness. Thus, they are intermediaries between our world and the next. Hearing the chants of life all around them, they are listeners who pass on the language and songs of many things to human beings who need wisdom, healing, and guidance through our lives, we who forget where we stand in the world. Bats know the world is constantly singing, know the world inside the turning and twisting of caves, places behind and beneath our own. As they scuttle across cave ceilings, they leave behind their scratch marks on the ceiling like an ancient alphabet written by diviners who traveled through and then were gone from the thirteen-month world of light and dark.

And what curing dwells at the center of this world of sounds above our own? Maybe it's as if earth's pole to the sky lives in a weightless cave, poking through a skin of dark and night and sleep.

At night, I see them out of the corner of my eye, like motes of dust, as secret as the way a neighbor hits a wife, a ghost cat slinks into a basement, or the world is eaten through by rust down to the very heart of nothing. What an enormous world. No wonder it holds our fears and desires. It is all so much larger than we are.

I see them through human eyes that turn around a vision, eyes that see the world upside down before memory rights it. I don't hear the high-pitched language of their living, don't know if they have sorrow or if they tell stories longer than a rainstorm's journey, but I see them. How can we get there from here, I wonder, to the center of the world, to the place where the universe carries down the song of night to our human lives. How can we listen or see to find our way by feel to the heart of every yes or no? How do we learn to trust ourselves enough to hear the chanting of earth? To know what's alive or absent around us, and penetrate the void behind our eyes, the old, slow pulse of things, until a wild flying wakes up in us, a new mercy climbs out and takes wing in the sky?

THE CAVES

EVENING ARRIVES AT THE MOUTH OF THE CAVE AND THE land turns blue. A soft mist is raining, the kind some call a female rain. Clouds rise up from where it touches ground. A creek moves through this place; it smells of iron and tastes of earth's blood. The land is open, receptive, and it is very young in terms of geological age, having just begun to move and shift. The elements of earth are patient and take their time to grow and collapse.

In earlier days, before the springs and caves were privately owned, they were places of healing for Indian people, places where conflict between tribes

and people was left behind, neutral ground, a sanctuary outside the reign of human differences, law,
and trouble. Men and women traveled across the
wide green plains, down the red mountains and
rounded hills, to rest inside earth's cauldron.

I WALK DOWN the passageway to inner earth. It is
almost dark inside this world's silent chambers, the
dank air warm and musty. Inside is a sacred place,
one of land's quiet temples where hot water journeys
upward after years of travel through deep earth. The
ceiling drips water, the slow sound of rain falling,
rhythmic, as if from the leaves of forests. In places,
the constant warm dripping of water has layed mineral down over rock, layer upon layer, until it is
smooth to the touch.

Barefoot, naked, I go down the stone pathway and
lower myself into the hot water. Surrounded by
stone, this body of mine is seen in the dim light for
what it is, fragile and brief. The water closes, seam-
less, around me. My foot with its blue-green veins is
vulnerable beside the rock-hard world that wants
someday to take me in. Can we love what will swallow us when we are gone? I do. I love what will consume us all, the place where the tunneling worms
and roots of plants dwell, where the slow deep centuries of earth are undoing and remaking themselves.

ONE TIME, WHEN I was a girl traveling with my family, we stopped to rest near the Continental Divide,
that place of separation where earth's water falls
away from itself. Drawn in by the solitude and

silence, I walked away from my family and wan-
dered about the land. Looking up, I saw a cave in the
rocks above me. Something moved there. As I looked
more closely, watching that movement, I saw that it
was a lion, not a mountain lion as might have been
expected, but an African lion. It wore a ragged mane
and looked out from the mouth of the cave. Its eyes
were gold and easy, its body lean and still. I turned
back, went to my father and told him, there is a lion,
an African lion, up there. He didn't believe me. He
climbed the hill, making his way up granite and
toward the cave in order to show me there was no
lion. He was young then, and agile.

I called him back away from the lion and danger,
but he went toward it.

While he climbed, the rest of my family ate. My
grandmother picked at a bone of chicken. But I
remained. I watched as my father reached the
entrance to the cave. He peered inside, then looked
at me and shook his head. No. There was no lion, no
wilderness with teeth and claws. But he did not go
in. He didn't enter the dark. When he returned, I
thought I smelled the odor of the lion on him. He
had not seen the lion, but it had seen him, and it
touched him, and I knew with certainty that it was
there.

I must have known, even then, that caves are not
the places for men. They are a feminine world, a
womb of earth, a germinal place of brooding. In
many creation stories, caves are the places that bring
forth life. In stories of the time before human time
and the people that lived before us, humans were said

to have come from a world beneath the one we now inhabit. They emerged from creation through caves. In a Cochiti Pueblo creation story, first man and first woman lived together inside a cave where they had planted game. Among the other kinds of animal life, they planted deer, rabbits, mountain lions, bear, and buffalo, and there the animals grew. In order to see them, the people first purified themselves in the steam heat of the caves, then they offered yellow pollen, and then, with a clear eye, they saw the animals walk out of the cave, emerge, the birds flying up into the haze of sky.

SINCE THAT TIME I've dreamed of caves. In one dream I passed through a doorway that was a gaping mouth, guarded by a skull. Light shone out from the eyes of that skull. Inside the cavern was warm, steaming water and chambers where women were working, sewing together bodies, stitching legs and arms, making life. I was there, in that dream, searching for my mothers: the earth, my human mother, my own life as a woman.

SUBMERGED IN THE hot water of this cave, I know this story; my blood remembers it. There is a different way of knowing here and I see all around me the constellations of animals. Rabbits are etched by minerals on wet stone walls. Deer are revealed in the moisture. Owls live inside the ceiling. In one corner of this cave is a puma. Salty blue minerals glitter across it. Clouds of steam rise up here. Two eagles perch in another dark chamber, watching and wait-

ing. There are the fetal beginnings of life to come, of
survival. I want this to be true. And I am not alone.
Another woman, purified by heat and steam, felt the
earth's heartbeat, heard the murmuring sounds of
breathing and shifting. That sharer in this world left
an offering of tobacco and sage. She knew these seeds
of life.

SEED. THERE ARE so many beginnings. In Japan, I
recall, there were wildflowers that grew in the far,
cool region of mountains. The bricks of Hiroshima,
down below, were formed of clay from these mountains, and so the walls of houses and shops held the
dormant trumpet flower seeds. But after one group
of humans killed another with the explosive power
of life's smallest elements split wide apart, the mountain flowers began to grow. Out of the crumbled,
burned buildings they sprouted. Out of destruction
and bomb heat and the falling of walls, the seeds
opened up and grew. What a horrible beauty, the
world going its own way, growing without us. But
perhaps this, too, speaks of survival, of hope beyond
our time.

   Some years ago, I came across a picture of an old,
thin Japanese woman. She had traveled to the broken city of Hiroshima after the bomb to find her
daughter and son-in-law. When she saw the suffering there, pain beyond the limits of human understanding, she turned away from her search and journeyed up into the hills. She remained in a cave,
alone, for over a year before she entered again the
world of people. She returned bony and wise. From

her eyes shone a light. She was the first woman to become a Shinto priest. What she knew she had learned from the cave, heard spoken by it, she had seen in the darkness.

IN 1981, IN Spain's Cantabrian Mountains, a cave was discovered that contained burnt offerings of red ocher, white clay, sewing needles of bone, and a stone carving thought to be a deity. On one side of it was the face of a man. On the other was the face of a lion. These were thought by the archaeologists to be representations of two natures—good and evil. They didn't say which was which. But it took me back to that day, traveling with my father. Years have passed; we have changed. He would understand that lion now, having grown old and returned to the inner world of his own self, as strong men do in their passage through life. There was something deeper than human that day, I think now, something of the world of myth. Now we are no longer at the divide, the place of separation. He would say now, I know, that a lion inhabits the cave.

OTHER women enter this cave and water. This time there are two other Indian women and a group of travelers from Japan. I want solitude, close my eyes, lower myself deeper in the water and try to enter my own silence. But then, something wonderful happens. A woman in one of the back chambers begins to sing, a long clear note that fills the whole tunnel. It echoes, an eerie, mysterious sound so that when she moves to another note, it sounds as if there are two voices, like the beautiful songs of humpback whales. Then, from the men's cave comes the howling of wolves. I think that these are the songs of lives struggling against extinction, even translated through human voices, they are here inside the earth, inside the human body, the captive, contained animals.

One of the Indian women talks about water medicine. She was sick and had lost her faith in the medicine ways, she says, and has come back to the healing waters of the earth.

We are welcome here. I love this inner earth, its murmuring heartbeat, the language of what will consume us. Above is the beautiful earth that we have come from. Below is heat, stone, fire. I am within the healing of nature, held in earth's hand.

ALL MY RELATIONS

IT IS A SUNNY, CLEAR DAY OUTSIDE, ALMOST HOT, AND A slight breeze comes through the room from the front door. We sit at the table and talk. As is usual in an Indian household, food preparation began as soon as we arrived, and now there is the snap of potatoes frying in the black skillet, the sweet smell of white bread overwhelming even the grease, and the welcome black coffee. A ringer washer stands against the wall of the kitchen, and the counter space is taken up with dishes, pans, and boxes of food.

I am asked if I still read books and I admit that I do. Reading is not "traditional" and education has long been suspect in communities that were broken, in part, by that system, but we laugh at my confession because a television set plays in the next room.

In the living room there are two single beds. People from reservations, travelers needing help, are frequent guests here. The man who will put together the ceremony I have come to request sits on one, dozing. A girl takes him a plate of food. He eats. He is a man I have respected for many years, for his commitment to the people, for his intelligence, for his spiritual and political involvement in concerns vital to Indian people and nations. Next to him sits a girl eating potato chips, and from this room we hear the sounds of the freeway.

After eating and sitting, it is time for me to talk to him, to tell him why we have come here. I have brought him tobacco and he nods and listens as I tell him about the help we need.

I know this telling is the first part of the ceremony, my part in it. It is story, really, that finds its way into language, and story is at the very crux of healing, at the heart of every ceremony and ritual in the older America.

The ceremony itself includes not just our own prayers and stories of what brought us to it, but also includes the unspoken records of history, the mythic past, and all the other lives connected to ours, our families, nations, and all other creatures.

I am sent home to prepare. I tie fifty tobacco ties, green. This I do with Bull Durham tobacco, squares of cotton that are tied with twine and left strung together. These are called prayer ties. I spend the time preparing alone and in silence. Each tie has a prayer in it. I will also need wood for the fire, meat and bread for food.

On the day of the ceremony, we meet in the next town and leave my car in public parking. My daughters and I climb into the backseat. The man who will help us is drumming and singing in front of us. His wife drives and chats. He doesn't speak. He is moving between the worlds, beginning already to step over the boundaries of what we think, in daily and ordinary terms, is real and present. He is already feeling, hearing, knowing what else is there, that which is around us daily but too often unacknowledged, a larger life than our own. We pass billboards and little towns and gas stations. An eagle flies overhead. It is "a good sign," we all agree. We stop to watch it.

We stop again, later, at a convenience store to fill the gas tank and to buy soda. The leader still drums and is silent. He is going into the drum, going into the center, even as we drive west on the highway, even with our conversations about other people, family, work.

It is a hot balmy day, and by the time we reach the site where the ceremony is to take place, we are slow and sleepy with the brightness and warmth of the sun. Others are already there. The children are cooling off in the creek. A woman stirs the fire that lives inside a circle of black rocks, pots beside her, a jar of oil, a kettle, a can of coffee. The leaves of the trees are thick and green.

In the background, the sweat lodge structure

stands. Birds are on it. It is still skeletal. A woman
and man are beginning to place old rugs and blan-
kets over the bent cottonwood frame. A great fire is
already burning, and the lava stones that will be the
source of heat for the sweat are being fired in it.

A few people sit outside on lawn chairs and cast-
off couches that have the stuffing coming out. We sip
coffee and talk about the food, about recent events.
A man tells us that a friend gave him money for a
new car. The creek sounds restful. Another man falls
asleep. My young daughter splashes in the water.
Heat waves rise up behind us from the fire that is
preparing the stones. My tobacco ties are placed
inside, on the framework of the lodge.

By late afternoon we are ready, one at a time, to
enter the enclosure. The hot lava stones are placed
inside. They remind us of earth's red and fiery core,
and of the spark inside all life. After the flap, which
serves as a door, is closed, water is poured over the
stones and the hot steam rises around us. In a sweat
lodge ceremony, the entire world is brought inside
the enclosure. The soft odor of smoking cedar accom-
panies this arrival. It is all called in. The animals
come from the warm and sunny distances. Water
from dark lakes is there. Wind. Young, lithe willow
branches bent overhead remember their lives rooted
in ground, the sun their leaves took in. They remember that minerals and water rose up their trunks, and
birds nested in their leaves, and that planets turned
above their brief, slender lives. The thunderclouds
travel in from far regions of earth. Wind arrives from
the four directions. It has moved through caves and

breathed through our bodies. It is the same air elk
have inhaled, air that passed through the lungs of a
grizzly bear. The sky is there, with all the stars whose
lights we see long after the stars themselves have
gone back to nothing. It is a place grown intense and
holy. It is a place of immense community and of
humbled solitude; we sit together in our aloneness
and speak, one at a time, our deepest language of
need, hope, loss, and survival. We remember that all
things are connected.

Remembering this is the purpose of the ceremony.
It is part of a healing and restoration. It is the mend-
ing of a broken connection between us and the rest.
The participants in a ceremony say the words "All
my relations" before and after we pray; those words
create a relationship with other people, with animals,
with the land. To have health it is necessary to keep
all these relations in mind. The intention of a ceremony is to put a person back together by restructur-
ing the human mind. This reorganization is accom-
plished by a kind of inner map, a geography of the
human spirit and the rest of the world. We make
whole our broken-off pieces of self and world. Within
ourselves, we bring together the fragments of our
lives in a sacred act of renewal, and we reestablish
our connections with others. The ceremony is a point
of return. It takes us toward the place of balance, our
place in the community of all things. It is an event
that sets us back upright. But it is not a finished
thing. The real ceremony begins where the formal
one ends, when we take up a new way, our minds
and hearts filled with the vision of earth that holds

us within it, in compassionate relationship to and with our world.

We speak. We sing. We swallow water and breathe smoke. By the end of the ceremony, it is as if skin contains land and birds. The places within us have become filled. As inside the enclosure of the lodge, the animals and ancestors move into the human body, into skin and blood. The land merges with us. The stones come to dwell inside the person. Gold rolling hills take up residence, their tall grasses blowing. The red light of canyons is there. The black skies of night that wheel above our heads come to live inside the skull. We who easily grow apart from the world are returned to the great store of life all around us, and there is the deepest sense of being at home here in this intimate kinship. There is no real aloneness. There is solitude and the nurturing silence that is relationship with ourselves, but even then we are part of something larger.

After a sweat lodge ceremony, the enclosure is abandoned. Quieter now, we prepare to drive home. We pack up the kettles, the coffeepot. The prayer ties are placed in nearby trees. Some of the other people prepare to go to work, go home, or cook a dinner. We drive. Everything returns to ordinary use. A spider weaves a web from one of the cottonwood poles to another. Crows sit inside the framework. It's evening. The crickets are singing. All my relations.

WHAT HOLDS THE WATER, WHAT HOLDS THE LIGHT

WALKING UP THE DAMP HILL IN THE HOT SUN, THERE were signs of the recent heavy rains. The land smelled fresh, shaded plants still held moisture in their green clustered leaves, and fresh deer tracks pointed uphill like arrows in the dark, moist soil.

Along our way, my friend and I stopped at a cluster of large boulders to drink fresh rain collected in a hollow bowl that had been worn into stone over slow centuries. Bending over the stone, smelling earth up close, we drank sky off the surface of water. Mosses and ancient lichens lived there. And swimming in another stone cup were slender orange newts, alive and vibrant with the rains.

Drinking the water, I thought how earth and sky are generous with their gifts, and how good it is to receive them. Most of us are taught, somehow, about giving and accepting human gifts, but not about opening ourselves and our bodies to welcome the sun, the land, the visions of sky and dreaming, not about standing in the rain ecstatic with what is offered.

One time, visiting friends, I found they had placed a Mexican water jar on the sink and filled it for me. It was a thin clay that smelled of dank earth, the unfired and unshaped land it had once been. In it was rain come from dark sky. A cool breeze lived inside the container, the way wind blows from a well that is held in the cupped hands of earth, fed with underground springs and rivers.

The jar was made in Mexico City, once called Iztapalapa, the place where Montezuma lived during the time Cortés and his Spanish soldiers were colonizing the indigenous people and the land. Writer Barry Lopez has written about the aviaries of Iztapalapa that were burned by the Spanish, fires that burned the green hummingbirds and nesting blue herons, burned even the sound of wings and the white songs of egrets. It was not only the birds that died in those fires, but also the people and their records, the stories of human lives.

De Soto also had this disregard for life. He once captured an indigenous woman because she carried a large pearl. His intention was, when they were far from her homeland, to kill the woman and steal the pearl, but one morning along their journey she managed to escape. De Soto's anger was enormous. It was as if the woman had taken something from him, and that fierce anger resulted in the killing of people and a relentless, ongoing war against land.

Humans colonizing and conquering others have a propensity for this, for burning behind them what they cannot possess or control, as if their conflicts are not with themselves and their own way of being, but with the land itself.

In the 1930s, looters found the Spiro burial mounds of Oklahoma and sold to collectors artifacts that they removed from the dead. When caught and forbidden to continue their thefts, the men dynamited two of the mounds the way a wolverine sprays food so that nothing else will take possession of it.

It seems, looking back, that these invasions amounted to a hatred of life itself, of fertility and generation. The conquerers and looters refused to participate in a reciprocal and balanced exchange with life. They were unable to receive the best gifts of land, not gold or pearls or ownership, but a welcome acceptance of what is offered. They did not understand that the earth is generous and that encounters with the land might have been sustaining, or that their meetings with other humans could have led to an enriched confluence of ways. But here is a smaller event, one we are more likely to witness as a daily, common occurrence. Last year, I was at the Colorado River with a friend when two men from the Department of Fish and Wildlife came to stock the water with rainbow trout. We wanted to watch the silver-sided fish find their way to freedom in the water, so we stood quietly by as the men climbed into

the truck bed and opened the tank that held fish. To
our dismay, the men did not use the nets they carried
with them to unload the fish. Instead they poured the
fish into the bed of their truck, kicked them out and
down the hill, and then into water. The fish that survived were motionless, shocked, gill slits barely moving, skin hanging off the wounds. At most, it would
have taken only a few minutes longer for the men to
have removed the fish carefully with their nets, to
have treated the lives they handled with dignity and
respect, with caretakers' hands.

These actions, all of them, must be what Bushman
people mean when they say a person is far-hearted.
This far-hearted kind of thinking is one we are especially prone to now, with our lives moving so quickly
ahead, and it is one that sees life, other lives, as containers for our own uses and not as containers in a
greater, holier sense.

Even wilderness is seen as having value only as it
enhances and serves our human lives, our human
world. While most of us agree that wilderness is necessary to our spiritual and psychological well-being, it
is a container of far more, of mystery, of a life apart
from ours. It is not only where we go to escape who
we have become and what we have done, but it is
also part of the natural laws, the workings of a world
of beauty and depth we do not yet understand. It is
something beyond us, something that does not need
our hand in it. As one of our Indian elders has said,
there are laws beyond our human laws, and ways
above ours. We have no words for this in our language, or even for our experience of being there.
Ours is a language of commerce and trade, of laws

that can be bent in order that treaties might be broken, land wounded beyond healing. It is a language
that is limited, emotionally and spiritually, as if it
can't accommodate such magical strength and power.
The ears of this language do not often hear the songs
of the white egrets, the rain falling into stone bowls.
So we make our own songs to contain these things,
make ceremonies and poems, searching for a new
way to speak, to say we want a new way to live in the
world, to say that wilderness and water, blue herons
and orange newts are invaluable not just to us, but in
themselves, in the workings of the natural world that
rules us whether we acknowledge it or not.

That clay water jar my friends filled with water
might have been made of the same earth that housed
the birds of Iztapalapa. It might have contained
water the stunned trout once lived in. It was not only
a bridge between the elements of earth, air, water,
and fire but was also a bridge between people, a
reservoir of love and friendship, the kind of care we
need to offer back every day to the world as we begin
to learn the land and its creatures, to know the world
is the container for our lives, sometimes wild and
untouched, sometimes moved by a caretaker's hands.
Until we learn this, and learn our place at the boun-
tiful table, how to be a guest here, this land will not
support us, will not be hospitable, will turn on us.

That water jar was a reminder of how water and
earth love each other the way they do, meeting at
night, at the shore, being friends together, dissolving
in each other, in the give and take that is where grace
comes from.

A DIFFERENT YIELD

*Hosanna! The corn reached total zenith in crested and entire
August. The space of summer arched earth to autumnal fruit.
Out of cold and ancient sod the split of protein, the primal
thunder. In the Mayan face of the tiny kernel look out the
deeps of time, space, and genes. In the golden pollen, more
ancient and fixed than the pyramids, is the scream of fleeing
Indians, germinal mirror of endurance, reflections of mothers
of different yield.*
——Meridel Le Sueur

A WOMAN ONCE DESCRIBED A FRIEND OF HERS AS BEING
such a keen listener that even the trees leaned toward
her, as if they were speaking their innermost secrets
into her listening ears. Over the years I've envisioned
that woman's silence, a hearing full and open enough
that the world told her its stories. The green leaves
turned toward her, whispering tales of soft breezes
and the murmurs of leaf against leaf.

When I was a girl, I listened to the sounds of the
corn plants. A breeze would begin in a remote corner
of the field and move slowly toward the closest edge,
whispering. After corn harvest at my uncle's farm,

the pigs would be set loose in the cornfield to feed on
what corn was left behind, kernels too dry for picking, too small for sale, or cobs that were simply
missed by human hands. Without a moment's hesi-
tation, the pigs would make straight for any plant
that still held an ear of corn, bypassing the others.
They would listen, it seemed, to the denser song of
corn where it still lived inside its dress of husk.

When I first heard of Barbara McClintock, it con-
firmed what I thought to be true about the language
of corn. McClintock is a biologist who received a
Nobel Prize for her work on gene transposition in
corn plants. Her method was to listen to what corn
had to say, to translate what the plants spoke into a
human tongue.

In *A Feeling for the Organism*, Evelyn Fox Keller
writes that McClintock came to know each plant intimately. She watched the daily green journeys of their
growth from earth toward sky and sun. She knew her
plants in the way a healer would know them, from
inside, from the inner voices of corn and woman. Her
approach to her science was alive, intuitive, and
humane. It was a whole approach, one that bridged
the worlds of woman and plant, and crossed over the
boundary lines between species. Her respect for life
allowed for a vision expanded enough, and sharp
enough, to see more deeply into the mysteries of matter than did other geneticists who were at work on
the same problems. Her revelation of method aston-
ished the scientific community. She saw an alive
world, a fire of life inside plants, even plants other
than the corn: "In the summertime, when you walk

down the road, you'll see that the tulip leaves, if it's a little warm, turn themselves around so their backs are toward the sun. Within the restricted areas in which they live, they move around a great deal. These organisms are fantastically beyond our wildest expectations."

In her book, *Adam's Task*, Vickie Hearne writes about the same kind of approach, only with animals, that McClintock used. She says there are things to be gained by respecting the intelligence of animals: "With horses, respect usually means respecting their nervousness, as in tales of retreating armies on horseback traversing minefields, in which the only riders who survive are the ones who gave their horses their heads, or tales of police horses who snort anxiously when a car in a traffic jam turns out to be carrying the thieves who escaped capture six months earlier."

These last years, it seems that much contemporary scientific exploration has been thrown full tilt into the center of one of those minefields, and is in search of a new vision, and of renewed intuitive processes of discovery that go beyond our previous assumptions about knowledge. This new requirement of thought turns out to be one that can only be called a leap of faith. "Over and over again," Keller says of McClintock, "she tells us one must have the time to look, the patience to 'hear what the material has to say to you. One must have a feeling for the organism.' "

A few years ago I was fortunate to meet a Jamaican artist named Everald Brown. Brown lives in a rural mountain town, one where houses have settled in with the enduring red earth. He creates carvings, paintings, and musical instruments that are radiantly alive with a resonance reaching far beyond the material, and far beyond the creations of most other artists who work with the same wood and pigment. Brown is what Jamaicans call an "intuitive artist," though he himself says only that the doves have taught him his craft. One of his intricately carved stringed instruments is painted with a blue sky. White, luminous doves are flying across it. And his wood carvings, made of lignum vitae, the tree of life, are rich with the lives of animals and birds emerging from the heavy center of wood.

Many creative people have called their inspiration "the muse." Often they say their ideas come from a spirit world, from a life other than their own human life. Even the Bible is a work so described by its authors; it is the voice of God.

Artist Paul Klee once said that we must return to the origins of things and their meanings, to the secret places where original law fosters all evolution, to the organic center of all movement in time and space, which is the mind or heart of creation.

This organic center, the center of creation, comes down to us through long traditions of learning the world's own songs. In American Indian traditions, healers are often called interpreters because they are the ones who are able to hear the world and pass its wisdom along. They are the ones who return to the heart of creation.

When we go back in human history, we find that it is not only the people now recognized as continuing in a tribal tradition who have known the voices of

earth, how corn both sings her own song and also
grows better with the songs and prayers of the people. Western traditions of consciousness also derive
from this approach to original, or aboriginal, ways of
knowing. Orpheus, for instance, was able to communicate with the worlds of animals, plants, water, and
minerals. Psyche, for whom psychology was named,
fell weeping on the ground, and while she was there
the ants offered a solution to the impossible task she
was assigned, that of separating a mountain of grain
before dawn. The river reeds also passed along their
secrets to Psyche, instructing her in the way to gather
wool from golden sheep.

From nearly all traditions, account after account
tells of stones giving guidance, as with Crazy Horse,
the Lakota prophet and politician who took his direction from a stone he wore beneath his arm. There are
tales of the trees singing, the corn that is called by
the Mayans "the grace," telling stories of inner earth.

In recent times, the term "myth" has come to sig-
nify falsehood, but when we examine myths, we find
that they are a high form of truth. They are the deepest, innermost cultural stories of our human journeys
toward spiritual and psychological growth. An essential part of myth is that it allows for our return to the
creation, to a mythic time. It allows us to hear the
world new again. Octavio Paz has written that in
older oral traditions an object and its name were not
separated. One equalled the other. To speak of corn,
for instance, was to place the corn before a person's
very eyes and ears. It was in mythic time that there
was no abyss between the word and the thing it

named, but he adds that "as soon as man acquired consciousness of himself, he broke away from the natural world and made himself another world inside himself."

This broken connection appears not only in language and myth but it also appears in our philosophies of life. There is a separation that has taken place between us and nature. Something has broken deep in the core of ourselves. And yet, there is another world created inside the person. In some way the balance between inner and outer worlds struggles to maintain itself in other and more complex ways than in the past. Psychologist C. A. Meier notes that as the wilderness has disappeared outside of us, it has gone to live inside the human mind. Because we are losing vast tracts of the wilderness, we are not only losing a part of ourselves, he says, but the threat to life which once existed in the world around us has now moved within. "The whole of western society," he says, "is approaching a physical and mental breaking point." The result is a spiritual fragmentation that has accompanied our ecological destruction.

In a time of such destruction, our lives depend on this listening. It may be that the earth speaks its symptoms to us. With the nuclear reactor accident in Chernobyl, Russia, it was not the authorities who told us that the accident had taken place. It was the wind. The wind told the story. It carried a tale of splitting, of atomic fission, to other countries and revealed the truth of the situation. The wind is a prophet, a scientist, a talker.

These voices of the world infuse our every act, as

much as does our own ancestral DNA. They give us back ourselves, point a direction for salvation. Sometimes they even shake us down to the bedrock of our own human lives. This is what I think happened in the 1970s language experiments in which chimpanzees were taught Ameslan, American Sign Language. In *Silent Partners,* Eugene Linden discusses the results of experiments with American Sign Language and chimpanzees. Probably the best known chimp is Washoe, a wild-caught chimpanzee who learned to use 132 signs, was able to ask questions and to use the negative. The book is extremely significant to our times, not because of what it tells us about apes and their ability to communicate in signs, so much as what it reveals about human beings and our relationships with other creatures.

The heated debates about the experiments came to revolve around whether or not it was actual language the chimps used. The arguments centered on definitions of language and intelligence, obscuring the real issue, that of how we treat other living beings. A reader comes to wonder how solid we are in the security of both ourselves and our knowledge when an issue of such significant scientific and spiritual importance sparks such a great division of minds, but if we are forced to accept that animals have intelligence, language, and sensitivity to pain, including psychological trauma, this acceptance has tremendous consequences for our own species and for our future actions.

While Linden says that "it is a little unsettling to be confronted with an animal who does not automatically acknowledge your paramountcy in the natural hierarchy," he also says that the experiments were disquieting not only because of the tragic consequences they created for the animals involved but because they also revealed the very fragile underpinnings of science. At the very least, the questions raised throughout this project were primarily questions about ourselves, our own morality, our way of being in the world, and our responsibility for the caretaking of the earth.

Vickie Hearne, on the same topic of language experiments, says we are facing an intellectual emergency. I want to take that word *emergency* a step further than the meaning it has come to hold for us, for this is not merely a crisis of the mind, but it is a potential act of emergence, of liberation for not only the animals of earth, but for our own selves, a freedom that could very well free us of stifling perceptions that have bound us tight and denied us the parts of ourselves that were not objective or otherwise scientifically respectable. When Linden notes that one of the chimp experimenters who came to care deeply for her subjects was outlawed from the world of science, I was reminded of how, during the 1970s when Harry Harlowe was conducting torturous research on chimps at the University of Wisconsin, one of the female students was found holding and comforting a chimp that was in pain. This act of compassion led Harlowe to conclude that there was a maternal instinct in women that kept them from objectivity, and that therefore they were not suited to the work of science. But even aside from that, the experiments were carried out to tell researchers what humans could have told them directly about their lives and needs, and not have been believed.

We have arrived despairingly at a time when compassion and care are qualities that do not lend themselves to the world of intellectual thought. Jimmie Durham, a Cherokee writer who was a prime mover in the development of an International Treaty Organization, wrote a poem called "The Teachings of My Grandmother," excerpted here:

> *In a magazine too expensive to buy I read about*
> *How, with scientific devices of great complexity,*
> *U.S. scientists have discovered that if a rat*
> *Is placed in a cage in which it has previously*
> *Been given an electrical shock, it starts crying.*
>
> *I told my grandmother about that and she said,*
> *"We probably knew that would be true."*

It might be that Linden comes close to the center of the dilemma about whether or not apes have language and intelligence when he says, "Perhaps it would be better to stick to figuring out the nature of stars and matter, and not to concern ourselves with creatures who threaten to paralyze us by shedding light on the true nature and origins of our abilities. Dismaying as this may sound, it is quite possible that we cannot afford to know who we are."

Not only have our actions revealed us to ourselves, and sometimes had dire results, but among many peoples educated in many European philosophical traditions, there is also an intense reaction to the bad news that cruelty is cruelty. There is a backlash effect that resists peacemaking. In 1986, I heard Betty Williams, a 1977 Nobel Peace Prize laureate from Northern Ireland, lecture in South Dakota. One afternoon Williams had witnessed the bombing death of Irish children. A little girl died in Williams's arms. The girl's legs had been severed in the explosion and had been thrown across the street from where the woman held the bleeding child. Williams went home in shock and despair. Later that night, when the shock wore off, the full impact of what she'd seen jolted her. She stepped outside her door, screaming out in the middle of the night. She knocked on doors that might easily have opened with weapons pointed at her face, and she cried out, "What kind of people have we become that we would allow children to be killed on our streets?" Within four hours the city was awake and there were sixteen thousand names on petitions for peace.

Williams's talk was interrupted at this point by a man who called out, "You're sick." Undisturbed by the heckler, Williams went on to tell how, touring the world as a peacemaker, she had left the starving people in Ethiopia for an audience with the pope. He told her, "I feel so worried about the hungry people," to which Williams responded, "Don't worry about them. Sell the Michelangelo and feed them."

Such a simple thing, to feed people. Such a common thing, to work for peace. Such a very clear thing, to know that if we injure an animal, ravage the land, that we have caused damage. And yet, we have rampant hunger and do not know, can hardly even imagine, peace. And even when animals learn to speak a language, and to communicate their misery, we still deny them the right to an existence free from suffering and pain.

I want to make two points here. One is about language and its power. While we can't say what language is much beyond saying that it is a set of signs and symbols that communicates meaning, we know it is the most highly regarded human ability. Language usage, in fact, often determines social and class order in our societal systems. Without language, we humans have no way of knowing what lies beneath the surface of one another. And yet there are communications that take place on a level that goes deeper than our somewhat limited human spoken languages. We read one another via gesture, stance, facial expression, scent. And sometimes this communication is more honest, more comprehensible, than the words we utter.

These inner forms of communication are perhaps the strongest core of ourselves. We have feelings that can't be spoken. That very speechlessness results in poems that try to articulate what can't be said directly, in paintings that bypass the intellectual boundaries of our daily vision, and in music that goes straight to the body. And there is even more a deep-moving underground language in us. Its currents pass between us and the rest of nature. It is the inner language that Barbara McClintock tapped for her research.

Hearne cites instances in which animals have

responded to these inner languages of people. The famous case of the horse Clever Hans is one of these. Hans was a horse that could do mathematical calculations and otherwise answer questions by tapping his hoof on the ground. As it turned out, Hans did not do the actual equations. Instead, he read the body language of the persons testing him. "Hans could always find out what the questioner thought was the correct answer, no matter how hard the questioner worked at remaining still and impassive. Hans apparently read minute changes in breathing, angles of the eyebrows, etc. with an accuracy we have trouble imagining." Hans's owner was denounced as a fraud. But, as Hearne points out, wasn't it a remarkable thing that the horse knew so well how to read people, even those other than his owner? They could not conceal from him the correct answer.

The critics of the ape language experiments worked vigorously to discredit the careful work of the researchers, and one of the variables they mentioned was this kind of unconscious leakage.

Another point that needs to be made is that when issues become obscured by distorted values or abstract concepts, we lose a clarity that allows us to act even in our own best behalf, for survival not just of ourselves but of the homeland which is our life and our sustenance. These responses stand in the way of freedom from pain. They obstruct the potentials we have for a better world. It is a different yield that we desire.

It must have been obvious at the inception of the language experiments that the work's very design was to determine whether or not a speaking ape might have a consciousness similar to that of a human. However, the results were distressing and the fate of the signing chimpanzees has been disastrous, some of them having been sold to research labs for other kinds of experimentation, including AIDS research.

We might ask what is to be gained by bridging the species gap? If it is, indeed, to determine intelligence levels, it seems that the talley on the side of the chimpanzees adds up to more points than ours, since the chimps are now bilingual. But, whatever the impetus, Linden says that the loser in the conflict concerning human and animal community is science. And while the chimps are the primary victims of this ongoing struggle, we also are "victims of a skewed view of our relationship with the rest of the natural order."

What we really are searching for is a language that heals this relationship, one that takes the side of the amazing and fragile life on our life-giving earth. A language that knows the corn, and the one that corn knows, a language that takes hold of the mystery of what's around us and offers it back to us, full of awe and wonder. It is a language of creation, of divine fire, a language that goes beyond the strict borders of scientific inquiry and right into the heart of the mystery itself. LeSueur writes: "Something enters the corn at the moment of fusion of the male and female that is unknown to scientists. From some star, a cosmic quickening, some light, movement-fast chemical that engenders illuminates quickens the conception, lights the fuse." Life itself, though we live it, is unknown to us. It is an alchemical process, a creative movement and exploration with the same magic in mind as the researchers had when they originated their search for meaning and relationship within the world.

We are looking for a tongue that speaks with reverence for life, searching for an ecology of mind. Without it, we have no home, have no place of our own within the creation. It is not only the vocabulary of science we desire. We want a language of that different yield. A yield rich as the harvests of earth, a yield that returns us to our own sacredness, to a self-love and respect that will carry out to others.

In most southwestern Indian cultures, the pollen of corn is sacred pollen. It is the life-giving seed of creation and fertility. Anthropologist Ruth Underhill wrote that Papago planters of corn would speak to the life-sustaining plants. "Night after night," she says, "the planter walks around his field, singing up the corn":

> *The corn comes up;*
> *It comes up green;*
> *Here upon our fields*
> *White tassels unfold.*
>
> *Blue evening falls;*
> *Blue evening falls;*
> *Near by, in every direction,*
> *It sets the corn tassels trembling.*

I know that corn. I know that blue evening. Those words open a door to a house we have always lived in.

Once, I ground corn with a smooth, round stone on

an ancient and sloping metate. Leaning over, kneeling on the ground, grinding the blue corn, seeing how the broken dry kernels turned soft, to fine meal, I saw a history in that yield, a deep knowing of where our lives come from, all the way back to the starch and sugar of corn.

She, the corn, is called our grandmother. She's the woman who rubbed her palms against her body and the seeds fell out of her skin. That is, they fell from her body until her sons discovered her secrets. Before she left the world, she told them how to plant. She said, plant the beans and corn together, plant their little sister, squash, between them. This, from an oral tradition, came to be rediscovered hundreds of years later, almost too late, by agriculturalists in their research on how to maintain the richness of farm soil.

Cherokee writer Carroll Arnett once gave me a bracelet of corn. There were forty-nine kernels, representing the number of clans, stitched round in a circle of life. I said, If I wear it when I die and am buried, won't it be wonderful to know that my life will grow up, out from beneath the earth? My life inside the green blades of corn, the stalks and tassels and flying pollen? That red corn, that corn will be this woman.

Imagine a woman, a scientist, listening to those rustling stalks, knowing their growth so intimately that "She could write the autobiography of every plant she worked with." What a harvest. What a different yield. In it is the pull of earth and life. The fields are beautiful.

Cornmeal and pollen are offered to the sun at dawn. The ears of the corn are listening and waiting.

They want peace. The stalks of the corn want clean water, sun that is in its full clean shining. The leaves of the corn want good earth. The earth wants peace. The birds who eat the corn do not want poison. Nothing wants to suffer. The wind does not want to carry the stories of death.

At night, in the cornfields, when there is no more mask of daylight, you hear the plants talking among themselves. The wind passes through. It's all there, the languages, the voices of wind, dove, corn, stones. The language of life won't be silenced.

In Chaco Canyon, in the center, my sister Donna told me, there is a kiva, a ceremonial room in the earth. This place has been uninhabited for what seems like forever. It has been without water so long that there are theories that the ancient people disappeared as they journeyed after water. Donna said that there was a corn plant growing out of the center of the kiva. It was alone, a single plant. It had been there since the ancient ones, the old ones who came before us all, those people who wove dog hair into belts, who witnessed the painting of flute players on the seeping canyon walls, who knew the stories of corn. There was one corn plant growing out of the holy place. It planted itself yearly. It was its own mother. With no water, no person to care for it, no turning over of the soil, this corn plant rises up. Earth yields. We probably knew that would be true.

Do you remember the friend that the leaves talked to? We need to be that friend. Listen. The ears of the corn are singing. They are telling their stories and singing their songs. We knew that would be true.

DEIFY THE WOLF

FEBRUARY IS SILENT, COLD, AND WHITE. ITS BLUE SHADOWS lie down on the north country's bare, icy winter. They call this region the Boundary Waters, and it is. It's the place where one country joins another, where bodies of land and water are broken by each other. The skeletal gray branches of trees define a terrain that is at the outermost limits of our knowledge and it is a shadowy world, one our bones say is the dangerous borderland between humans and wilderness.

In winter when cold and water marry, this region becomes a horizon of ice. Now and then, a moose, hungry enough to venture across the glare ice from one island to another, becomes stranded in the slippery dark center of these frozen waters and has no choice but to remain still until the weather changes. Wolves are at an advantage here; they move easily over the shining passages from one piece of land to another. These are their pathways, and a stranded moose is often their weather-snared prey.

ALL OF US who are here in Ely, Minnesota, studying wolves have followed some inner impulse to this cold region. We have come here to search for timber wolves, those howling ones the Anishnabe people say human beings descended from long ago, back in the days when animals and people spoke the same tongue. Anyone who has heard the howl of wolves breaking through a northern night will tell you that a part of them still remembers the language of that old song. It stirs inside the body, taking us down from our world of logic, down to the deeper lost regions of ourselves into a memory so ancient we have lost the name for it.

One man has come because he wants to see the threatened wolves before they are extinct. A California woman thinks seeing the wolves would be "like in the movies." Another man is a trapper who earns $1,500 a year trapping fur animals and says he'll hunt and trap as long as women will wear fur coats.

I can't say why I am here, but I have followed a map in the blood, an instinct I don't know. I think of my daughter who, never having heard a wolf, one day sang just like one, and we now say of Tanya that she has wolfblood. And an Anishnabe boy in Minneapolis, Jim Larsen, said in his poem: "I'm Indian because the wolf howls my name in the night." I think this is so with me, at least in part.

No matter the reason we say we are here, all of us are intent on seeing the wolves, or hearing them wail the song our ancestors knew the words to. We are looking for the clue to a mystery, a relative inside our own blood, an animal so equal to us that it reflects back what we hate and love about ourselves.

What we see of the wolves may be only the remains of a moose, its walled open rib cage rising out from snow that's red with the bloody signs of struggle. Or we might see nothing more than a group of gypsy ravens flying across the white sky, crying out that the wolf pack on earth beneath them has made a kill. The birds are companions of the wolves. It is thought that they direct the wolves to their prey, then stand by until the carcass is relinquished to them for their own earned share in the feast. Occasionally, a person happens across a coal black raven standing inside the wide arch of those ribs like a soul in a body.

THIS NORTH COUNTRY is a place desolate and ransacked by those who have tried to survive here. The land cries out the thefts that have taken place. A once-tall canopy of Norway pines has been gone since loggers, new to the Americas, carried the trees across the country to be transformed into houses and barns that, in early days, I'm told, were painted red with a mixture of milk and the red blood of slaughtered cattle. There are evergreens here, and thin, spare birch with cracks that look like dark eyes staring out of their white trunks. Wind rattles their loose, papery bark on these cold winter days, and the frozen world seems full of the voices of spirits.

The lives of wolves and men have crossed one another often in this northern land. Fortunes grew from the trapped spoils of beaver, wolf, and fox. Not long ago, there were the mines; iron rose up out of earth and traveled across the continent. It became metal shoes on workhorses. It was turned into bars for jails. It became leg traps for the bears who were once plentiful here. What a strange alchemy we have worked, turning earth around to destroy itself, using earth's own elements to wound it.

A holdover from the iron mining days is "the dump pack," a group of wolves that grew accustomed to the presence of miners and were tame enough to accept balogna sandwiches from the men's hands. While the other packs steered away from human contact, what remains of the dump pack still pilfers food from what people have discarded.

Recently the lives of wolves and men have begun to cross in new ways. A group of wildlife biologists is here to conduct a study of wolf populations. It's an uncomfortable situation. The townspeople, uncertain about what the biologists are up to, worry that they are here to save the wolves. Concerned that they are "environmentalists," they complain that the researchers want to "Deify the wolf," to make it holier, they say, than the sacred cow of India, a perception both extreme and irrational.

The conflict is a long-term one. It is based on

beliefs that wolves and humans, both predators, are in competition with one another for food and territory. Local residents wonder if their children are safe with wolves living in the outlying regions of their own lots and invisible property lines. It doesn't matter that the tension between locals and what they think of as "environmentalists," or wolf-lovers, begins to wedge apart the two groups in much the way that a split has widened between so many European immigrants and the American wilderness they have never been at home with.

The local sentiment "there is no wolf like a dead wolf" does not seem likely to change, no matter what the researchers find, and there is very little assurance that this last substantial population of timber wolves will survive. The leading cause of death for wolves is contact with the human world. Our presence means tragedy to them. They are shot by hunters, trapped, poisoned, and hit by logging trucks as they travel the human roads.

Not long ago, it was legal to shoot wolves from airplanes. Wolves at rest after eating, or sunning themselves in the rare warmth of daylight, were gunned down by men who leaned out the windows of their small planes. Both Minnesota and Canada paid bounty for the hides. Farley Mowatt, in his book *Never Cry Wolf*, writes of the horrors, committed against wolves, the slaughters, the human hunters who blamed many of their own mutilations of other animals on packs of wolves in order to justify the "revenge" killings of the wolf.

Not long ago in this area, trappers used strychnine

in the carcasses of animals, poisoning not only wolves but also birds, lynx, and other animals. In South Dakota, where wolves once flourished, a starving group of Nakota Indians was killed by the strychnine intended for wolves; government commodities that had been promised as payment for Indian land did not arrive as promised by treaty, and the people were forced to scavenge from the land. The land there, once Indian land, grazed by cattle ranchers, was no longer productive for wildlife or food. The people, hungry, were forced to eat meat that had been set out for wolves, and they met with the same miserable fate.

CONDUCTING RESEARCH ORIGINATED by L. David Mech, the biologists have devised a modified version of the steel-jaw leg traps in order to immobilize the wolves for study. For utmost safety, the teeth of the traps are sawed off so that the jaws don't quite come together. There are casualties; a frantic wolf, fearful, chews a stick that is in the trap. The stick wedges in its mouth. The wolf starves, which means he has been forgotten long enough to die of hunger. Or, desperate for freedom, another trapped wolf, intelligent enough to comprehend the future, desperately chews off its leg and leaves it in the trap. There is a mystique about these wolves that lose a leg. Because they fight for life, they are worthy of human respect. They are called "Ghost Leg" and "Phantom" and other names that give these wolves significance because they want to live and we can identify with that; these wounded wolves are like us, freedom and life mean

something to them, something important, as it does
to us.

When a wolf is trapped by the biologists, blood
samples are taken, the animal identified, and a radio
telemetry collar is buckled into place. The collar
allows the biologists to follow the wolves by radar.
They are tracked throughout their territories, often
from a small plane. Inside the collar is a dart that
contains a tranquilizer ampule. It can be fired into
the neck of the wolf from afar when researchers find
it necessary to tranquilize and capture one of their
subjects. There are casualties here, also, such as the
time a wolf lost consciousness in water and drowned.

The packs here have learned to chew collars off
one another. According to biologists, one pack even
taught a second pack how this was done. As they said
this, there was again a tone of admiration in their
voices, a respect for the intelligence of wolves.

A few of us wonder if the interference of this study
isn't as bad for the wolves as the ongoing presence of
hunters and trappers has been. The biologists share
that concern. One of them points out how the study
of California condors created stress levels so high that
many of the birds died as a direct result of the study.
We are in a double bind here. So are the wolves. No
matter how we look at it, this is a difficult and pre-
carious predicament. It seems that we have created a
world for ourselves where all of our actions have dire
consequences in a way reminiscent of federal Indian
policies. Still, despite the deaths resulting from this
study, the hope is that the final outcome will be one
of long-term survival for wolves.

But some of the findings have already been significant in dispelling many of the myths about wolves. For instance, wolves have long been blamed for the decrease in deer populations, but the researchers have found that hunters in Minnesota shoot 100,000 deer a year, while the wolf kills total only 18,000. In the Duluth and Cloquet area, the researchers noted, as many as fifty deer a day are killed by domestic dogs, a very significant finding. The biologists also have found that domestic animals are rarely killed by wolves, but because they will scavenge a dead cow or sheep, people have been misled to think the wolves were responsible for the deaths.

ONE OF THE biologists brings several wolf carcasses from the back of his pickup for us to examine. As usual when death lies before us, we find ways to hide our vulnerability. The trapper among us points at one of the dead wolves and says, "Put my name on it." Then he holds up a young wolf, one that had starved, and asks another member of our group to take a photograph of him holding it. He first brushes the dirt off its fur, so it will "look like I caught it."

I can tell a few of the other people share my discomfort about the man's behavior, but they laugh. Like the wolves, we humans are social animals and hide our feelings in tense situations.

One of the wolves was hit by a truck. I examine one that had starved to death. I see that it has been caught in a leg-hold trap. The biologist, who said merely that it starved, is young and embarrassed when I ask about the injury. He tells us the snare was the reason why the pup starved to death. It wasn't a wolf trap, he assures us, but a fox trap. The dishonesty interests me but he is in a difficult position. His tact, his opinion on either side, is liable to have a serious effect on the lives of wolves. Environmental work, like tribal issues have been for us Indian people, is subject to very negative reactions, to what we call "backlash." This situation is especially fragile, complicated by the psychological fact that wolves carry much of the human shadow. They contain for us many of our own traits, ones we repress within ourselves. More than any other animal, they mirror back to us the predators we pretend not to be. In that way, we have assigned to them a special association with evil.

Close up, there is even more beauty in the wolf than any of us have seen from a distance. The fur is shadowy gray and golden. The jawbones with their circular valleys are smooth, outlined by the bare, lean winter. Inside the mouth, the teeth are layered and worn down. There are strawberry leaves, frozen in place, on the wolf's teeth at the gum line. The tenderness of such an image moves me. I feel it in the heart. And there is something delicate about the legs, something gone from wandering earth, something that ran so far it left the body behind.

What part of this appeals to the people, I wonder, surely not an odor of death on their hands, though they want to touch the wolves, and despite the −20 temperature, they remove their gloves to do so.

I saw in a Colorado newspaper a picture of a young woman walking a captive black wolf on a leash. Its narrow body was tight, pulled in, its gold eyes looked wild and afraid. People passing by on the street had stopped to touch it, smiling at it, speaking. What did they want to touch or to have touch them? The hand is our contact with the world of other species, the sense we have that most arouses the feeling in us of being moved and touched. I'm reminded of the day a fawn arrived at the wildlife clinic where I worked. It was tiny and golden, its slender legs curled up beneath it on the examining table. Everyone came to see it, everyone's hands touching the soft fur of the terrified, dark-eyed deer. What need we humans have, a species lonely and lacking in love. These are gestures reserved for animals because the distance between one human and another is often too great to bridge.

Our loneliness and lack of compassion are noted by others. Mother Teresa trained some of her apprentices to work in North American cities rather than in Calcutta. Her followers preferred Calcutta because, as Mother Teresa said, the suffering of loneliness in the United States was more painful to bear than the daily deaths from hunger and disease in India. Perhaps it is because of that loneliness that we remove our gloves in icy weather to touch a dead wolf.

One man photographs the other holding the dead wolf on its legs, as if it is still alive. This picture is something for the man to keep, a connection to something he needs. He, like the others, wants to touch a lost piece of the wild earth. Another picture is taken, this time of a man holding the wolf up by its ears. He says the wolf head would be good to put on a walking stick. And I see the wolf invaded even in death as the men touch it, rearrange it, and note that "he doesn't have a nose."

This show takes my memory to other times and places. I remember the dentist who proudly used the skull of Chief Joseph as an ashtray; the military men who were part of the Sand Creek massacre and who pinned the innermost parts of Indian women's bodies to their hat and over their saddlehorns. I remember, too, the account of the survivors, who felt such grief that their women and children and elders were killed that they cut themselves, trying to die, weeping.

I'VE WORKED WITH death and I respect it, so it is hard to understand these human beings, let alone come close to knowing the inner terrain of the wolf. I believe people fear their own deaths, so they must belittle it. There are lessons to be learned in our behavior.

I realize now that I won't learn about the wolves, our ancestors from before history. They are too complex for that. I can only return to the way people wanted to touch the fawn and these wolves. Something wild must hold such sway over the imagination that we can't tear ourselves away from any part of wilderness without in some way touching it.

IT IS MORNING, and snowing heavily. The wind lifts the snow up above the trees.

Later, when the snow stops, it is my turn to enter the small propellor airplane. It's noisy, whirring, and clattering. It has landed in the middle of frozen

water. I walk out, move beneath the wind of the propellor, and climb up into the plane.

As we lift up, there's the shock of separation.
Uprooted from land, at first it is frightening. But
once in the air it is comfortable, somehow even comforting.

The snow has covered the tracks of wolves, so
there is no easy path toward them. We fly over island
after island in the cold white world. From sky, the
country is wide and beautiful. It is more spare than a
person could guess from the ground.

Then, three wolves. They are curled up like dogs,
sleeping beside the enormous moose they have killed.
They are full and lazy. The crows are there, on the
carcass. The wolves look like gray shadows. They
don't look up at us or move away. They have forgotten, or they have given up.

Flying above them this way is like being part of a
destruction I don't want to believe in. Swedish poet
Sandro Key-Aberg says: "It is the animal that brings
us together, it is the human that separates us."

This plane is part of the human. It is part of separation.

IN THE ASH gray world of evening, the sky turns
black. This far into the animal we find the human,
and this far into the human we find the animal.
Thinking long and hard about wolves, I feel as if
they have possessed me—taken me in. I feel lost,
transported. It's night. Most of the human machines
are silent. The ice cracks. A slow moaning is deep
inside it. The trees are creaking in the wind. It is dark
and cold. The birch bark rattles.

We are outside. We are silent, listening to the sounds that are all around us. We are small in this large, cold land. It feels like something else is here, the way it does in solitude when a person faces their own life in the night and turns in, toward their own dark wilderness. It's as if something old, some secret thing that has gone before us, returns in the moonscape and luminous snow. Alone here, any one of us would know a rushing fear.

We are walking the road near the dump. We are quiet. I'm thinking of how the elaborate ritual of one wolf greeting another is called a ceremony. It's ceremony we want a share of. We are walking here to speak with the wolves. That's what we want. We want to reach out to them, to tell them we are here. We want them to answer, acknowledge us, maybe even to like us. We think they will see our souls.

We walk. None of us speak. We are listening for a howl. We want to hear it traveling in from the outer edge of the forest.

I look up. The sky is shimmering. If we could hear it, we'd know the sky is howling and its cry is spreading wide across the darkness. I have never seen the northern lights before. The sky is filled with them. They are dancing, the color of roses, the green of springtime. The lights shimmer and move around the black dome of sky. The Anishnabe call them dancing ghosts.

Surrounding us are the trees, the shadowy world of wolves. Magic is above us. Underneath us, beneath these lakes and islands, is some of the oldest rock in the world, more than three billion years old. In places, the iron is so concentrated in the underlying stone that the needle of the compass points away from magnetic north.

You could say this strange place has its own north, a pull of its own. I feel it tugging down the bones and muscles. There's a fire beneath the land, farther down in the molten core, a heat at dead center, and even the dust from solar storms moves toward it.

We walk up the road. None of us speak. Then there is the howl. It is soft and long. Even the loose skin of the trees holds still. Everything listens. There is another slow, rising howl. It is a man. It's a man speaking. In a language he only pretends to know, he calls out to the wolves.

We wait. We are waiting for the wolves to answer. We want a healing, I think, a cure for anguish, a remedy that will heal the wound between us and the world that contains our broken histories. If we could only hear them, the stars themselves are howling, but there is just the man's voice, crying out, lonely. Not even those of us standing behind him answer. It is a silence we rarely feel, a vast and inner silence that goes deep, descends to the empty spaces between our cells. The dancing ghosts still linger above us. I know this woeful song. I have heard it before. I have heard women wail this way in grief, heard the wild, lonely song rage up a rising scale of sorrow.

We have followed the wolves and are trying to speak across the boundaries of ourselves. We are here, and if no wolf ever answers, or even if no wolves remained, we'd believe they are out there. And they are.

CREATIONS

"We were told by the Creator, This is your land. Keep it for me until I come back."

—Thomas Banyaca, Hopi elder

WE ARE TRAVELING TOWARD THE END OF LAND, TO A place called Ria de Celestun, Estuary of Heaven. It is a place where clouds are born. On some days they rise up above the river and follow water's path. On those days, from across the full length of land, Rio Esperanza, the River of Hope, can be seen as it is carried up into the sky. But today, the late morning clouds have formed farther out, above the ocean.

It is the day after spring equinox, and as we near the ocean, whiteness is the dominant feature. Salt beds stretch out at water's edge. Beaches, made of sea-worn limestone and broken-down coral, are nearly blinding in the early spring light. Water, itself, wears the sun's light on its back, and near a road sign several young men are at work, throwing buckets of salt-dried fish into the bed of a pickup truck.

It has been a long, narrow road through the Yucatán. We have passed jungle, brush, and villages created from bone-colored limestone. A woman in an embroidered white Hupil walks along the road carrying a bundle of firewood. Smoke from a household fire rises above the thatched roofs. Two boys with small rifles step into the forest in search of food. In spite of the appearance of abundance in the Yucatán, it is a world endangered, not only by deforestation, but also by other stresses to the environment, by human poverty. It is a hungry place with dwindling resources.

In some villages, the few livestock—a single horse, a solitary cow—are bony of rib. People, too, in many towns are thin with a poverty that as it grows diminishes the world about it.

Many of the people in and near Ria de Celestun are new people. Previously, they were farmers of henequen, a plant used to make hemp rope, but since the introduction of plastic and nylon rope, the people have been relocated without consideration for what their presence would mean in this region, or how they would stretch a living out of the land. In order to build houses, swamps were filled in with garbage. There are sewage problems and contaminated water, and the cutting of trees has destroyed the watershed. With the close-in waters now overfished, the farmers-turned-fishermen are forced into the dangerous business of taking poorly equipped boats out to deeper waters in search of food.

In geological history, as with that of the people, this is a place of rising and collapsing worlds. There is constant movement and transformation. Some are subtle changes, the way mangrove swamps create new soil, the way savannah grows from the fallen mangrove leaves, but most of the boundaries here are crossed in sudden and dramatic ways, the result of the elemental struggle between water and land, where a water-shaped cave collapses and new water surges to fill the sinkhole left behind, where water claims its edges from land, where swamp becomes ocean, ocean evaporates and leaves salt. The land itself bears witness to the way elements trade places; it is limestone that floated up from the sea, containing within it the delicate, complex forms of small animals from earlier times; snails, plants, creatures that were alive beneath water are still visible beneath the feet. To walk on this earth is to walk on a living past, on the open pages of history and geology.

Now even the dusty road we travel becomes something else as it disappears into the ocean at Celestun. It is a place of endings and of beginnings, full with the power of creation.

Holy Mother Earth, the trees and all nature, are
witnesses of your thoughts and deeds.
                                        —Winnebago

For the Maya, time was born and had a name when
the sky didn't exist and the earth had not yet awak-
ened.

The days set out from the east and started walking.

The first day produced from its entrails the sky and the earth.

The second day made the stairway for the rain to run down.

The cycles of the sea and the land, and the multitude of things, were the work of the third day.

The fourth day willed the earth and the sky to tilt so that they could meet.

The fifth day decided that everyone had to work.

The first light emanated from the sixth day

In places where there was nothing, the seventh day put soil; the eighth plunged its hands and feet in the soil.

The ninth day created the nether worlds; the tenth earmarked for them those who had poison in their souls.

Inside the sun, the eleventh day modeled stone and tree.

It was the twelfth that made the wind. Wind blew, and it was called spirit because there was no death in it.

The thirteenth day moistened the earth and kneaded the mud into a body like ours.

Thus it is remembered in Yucatán.

—Eduardo Galeano

Inside people who grow out of any land there is an understanding of it, a remembering all the way back to origins, to when the gods first shaped humans out of clay, back to when animals could speak with people, to when the sky and water were without form and all was shaped by such words as *Let there be.*

In nearly all creation accounts, as with the Maya,

life was called into being through language, thought, dreaming, or singing, acts of interior consciousness. For the Maya, time itself is alive. In the beginning, the day sets out walking from the east and brings into being the world and all that inhabited it, jaguar, turtle, deer, trees. It was all sacred.

Then there were the first humans, whose job it was to offer prayer, tell stories, and remember the passage of time. Made of the clay of this earth, the mud people of the first creation did not endure; when it rained, their bodies grew soft and dissolved.

In the next creation, humans were lovingly carved of wood. These prospered and multiplied. But in time, the wooden people forgot to give praise to the gods and to nurture the land. They were hollow and without compassion. They transformed the world to fit their own needs. They did not honor the sacred forms of life on earth, and they began to destroy the land, to create their own dead future out of human arrogance and greed. Because of this, the world turned against them. In a world where everything was alive, the forms of life they had wronged took vengeance on them. There was black rain. The animals they harmed attacked them. The ruined waters turned against them and flooded their land.

In the final creation of mankind, the people were created from corn:

> *And so then they put into words the creation,*
> *The shaping of our first mother*
> *And father.*
> *Only yellow corn*
> *And white corn were their bodies.*

Only food were the legs
And arms of man.
Those who were our first fathers
Were the original men.
Only food at the outset
Were their bodies.
—from the Quiche Maya, Popul Vuh

At first, these care-taking, life-giving people made of corn, the substance of gods, saw what the gods saw. In order to make them more human, less godlike, some of this vision was taken away so there might be mystery, and the mystery of creation and of death inspired deep respect and awe for all of creation.

In most stories of genesis, unwritten laws of human conduct are taught at creation. For the Maya, too, the story of the hollow people is not only part of a beautiful and complex creation story but also a telling language, one that speaks against human estrangement from land.

Emptiness and estrangement are deep wounds, strongly felt in the present time. We have been split from what we could nurture, what could fill us. And we have been wounded by a dominating culture that has feared and hated the natural world, has not listened to the voice of the land, has not believed in the inner worlds of human dreaming and intuition, all things that have guided indigenous people since time stood up in the east and walked this world into existence, split from the connection between self and land.

The best hunters of the far north still find the

location of their prey by dreaming. In *Maps and Dreams,* by anthropologist Hugh Brody, one informant says, "Maybe you don't think this power is possible. Few people understand. The old-timers who were strong dreamers knew many things that are not easy to understand. . . . The fact that dream-hunting works has been proved many times." Maps of the land and the direction of deer are revealed in dreams.

Like the wooden people, many of us in this time have lost the inner substance of our lives and have forgotten to give praise and remember the sacredness of all life. But in spite of this forgetting, there is still a part of us that is deep and intimate with the world. We remember it by feel. We experience it as a murmur in the night, a longing and restlessness we can't name, a yearning that tugs at us. For it is only recently, in earth time, that the severing of the connections between people and land have taken place. Something in our human blood is still searching for it, still listening, still remembering. Nicaraguan poet-priest Ernesto Cardenal wrote, "We have always wanted something beyond what we wanted." I have loved those words, how they speak to the longing place inside us that seeks to be whole and connected with the earth. This, too, is a place of beginning, the source of our living.

So also do we remember our ancestors and their lives deep in our bodily cells. In part, this deep, unspoken remembering is why I have come to the Yucatán, searching out my own beginnings, the thread of connection between old Maya cultures and my own Chickasaw heritage. According to some of our oral traditions, a migration story of our tribe, we originated in this region, carved dugout canoes, and traveled to the southeast corner of what is now called Florida, the place of flowers. I have always felt a oneness with this Mexican land, but I know this call to origins is deeper, older, and stronger than I am, more even than culture and blood origins. Here, there is a feel for the mystery of our being in all ways, in earth and water. It is a feel for the same mystery that sends scientists to search for the beginning of the universe. We seek our origins as much as we seek our destinies.

And we desire to see the world intact, to step outside our emptiness and remember the strong currents that pass between humans and the rest of nature, currents that are the felt voice of land, heard in the cells of the body.

It is the same magnetic call that, since before human history, has brought the sea turtles to the beach of Celestun. The slow blood of the turtles hears it, turtles who have not been here since the original breaking of the egg that held them, who ran toward an ocean they did not know, who have lived their lives in the sea then felt the call of land in deep memory and so return to a place unseen. Forever, it seems, they have been swimming through blue waters in order to return, to lay their eggs in sun-warmed sand, and go back to the clear blue-green waters of their mothers in ancient journeys of creation and rituals of return.

THE WHITE SHORELINE stretches around us, wide and open. It is early for the endangered hawksbills and green turtles to be coming to land. Egg laying usually begins in late April and early May. Because of the endangered status of the sea turtles, members of an organization called Pronatura will arrive to protect the turtles and the eggs. In this region in 1947, there were so many sea turtles that it was said 40,000 of them appeared on one beach to spawn. Now the hawksbills are the second most endangered species in the world. Today, despite the earliness of the season, there are tracks in the white sand, large tracks that have moved earth as if small tanks had emerged from the water and traveled a short distance up sand. Some of the tracks return, but others vanish, and where they end, there are human footprints.

IN THE TRADITIONAL BELIEF systems of native people, the terrestrial call is the voice of God, or of gods, the creative power that lives on earth, inside earth, in turtle, stone, and tree. Knowledge comes from, and is shaped by, observations and knowledge of the natural world and natural cycles.

In fact, the word *God* in the dictionary definition means to call, to invoke. Like creation, it is an act of language, as if the creator and the creation are one, the primal pull of land is what summons.

Sometimes beliefs are inventions of the mind. Sometimes they are inventions of the land. But how we interpret and live out our lives has to do with the religious foundations and the spiritual history we have learned.

The Western belief that God lives apart from earth is one that has taken us toward collective destruction. It is a belief narrow enough to forget the value of matter, the very thing that soul inhabits. It has created a people who neglect to care for the land for the future generations.

The Lakota knew that man's heart, away from nature, becomes hard; he knew that lack of respect for growing, living things soon led to lack of respect for humans, too.
—Luther Standing Bear

Not far from here is where Fray Diego de Landa, in the 1500s, tortured and killed the Maya people and burned their books in the alchemical drive of the Spanish to accumulate wealth, turn life into gold, and to convert others to their own beliefs. They set into flames entire peoples and centuries of remembered and recorded knowledge about the land. It is believed that there were considerable stores of knowledge in these people and in their books, not just history and sacred stories but medical knowledge, a math advanced enough to create the concept of zero, and a highly developed knowledge of astronomy whose intelligence continues to surprise contemporary astronomers. It is certain that centuries of habitation on this land yielded more knowledge about the earth and its cycles than has been newly understood and recovered in the brief, troubled years that have since followed. And we are left to wonder if that ancient knowledge would help us in this time of threat, if the lost books held a clue to survival.

This burned and broken history is part of the story of the land. It is the narrative of the past by which we still live. But the memory of an older way remains. It is stored in the hearts and blood of the people and in the land. Fray de Landa for one brief moment acknowledged such life when he wrote that this land is "the country with the least earth that I have ever seen, since all of it is one living rock." These words, this recognition of living rock, might have bridged a different connection, an understanding closer to the way indigenous people see the land, and a life-sustaining way of being.

The tides are always shifting things about among the mangrove roots.... Parts of it are neither land nor sea and so everything is moving from one element to another.
                                    —Loren Eiseley, *Night Country*

A rib of land separates ocean and barrier beach from the red-colored tidal estuary and wetlands area where the river runs toward larger waters. The river is so full of earth that it is red and shallow. In its marshy places, plants grow from its clay. There are places where freshwater underground rivers surge upward to create conditions that exist nowhere else.

There is salt marsh, a tidal estuary, and mangrove swamps that contain one of the world's largest colonies of flamingos, birds named after flame, as if they belong, in part, to the next element of creation. This red estuary is alive and breathing, moving with embryonic clay and silt.

It is a place crucial not only to the flamingo colonies and waterfowl but also to migratory birds from as far north as Maine, a connection that closes the miles, another boundary undone.

Traveling into this red water, we are surrounded by the many-rooted mangrove swamps. Mangroves, a network of tangled roots and twisted branches, are a part of creation and renewal in this land. Coastal plants, they live in the divide between land and water. Both marine and terrestrial, these plants are boundary-bridgers that have created islands and continents. Consuming their own fallen leaves, they are nurturers in the ongoing formation of the world, makers of earth, and the mangroves have a life force strong enough to alter the visible face of their world. Rachel Carson called them a world "extending back into darkening swamps of its own creation."

The interior of the swamps is dark and filled with the intricate relationships of water with plant, animal, earth, sheltering small lives within them.

Mangroves are plants that reach out to grow, searching for water and minerals with a grasping kind of energy that can be felt. As they send their roots seeking outward, they move forward, leaving behind them the savannah that will become tropical forest. In turn, rainwater flowing underground will break through the forest and create a cenote. No one knows the paths of these rivers. Theirs is a vast underground network. It is only known where they rise. And in some of these sinkholes, or cenotes, are species of fish from one river system not found in other cenotes in the region.

The rain clouds have not yet reached us. Light shines through the leaves. A fish jumps. As we move forward, the path of our disturbance is lighter in color, like a vapor trail, behind us. Then it vanishes, unlike the paths we have left behind in other places. There is a dreaminess here where creation continues to happen all around us in time that is alive.

AT THE FAR edge of copper-colored water, a white egret steps through the shallows, an eye sharp for fish. On the other side of water's edge stands a solitary blue heron. Herons are fragile birds, and it is not unusual for them to die from stress. I think of them when hearing that Hmong men, forced to leave their country and rootless in America, die of no apparent cause while they are sleeping. I understand the loss that leads to despair and to death. It has happened to us and is happening to land, the breaking of the heart of creation.

The poet Gertrud Kolmar, a woman who loved animals, died in Auschwitz, one of those lost by whatever other failures of the gods have made men hollow and capable of such crimes. There is a poem of hers that herons fly through. With rigid legs and boomerang wings they fly beneath rolling clouds through a smoke blue sky, flying toward dawn, flying without falling from heaven. But the holocaust began before her time. It began on this continent, with the genocide of tribal people, and with the ongoing war against the natural world. Here is a lesson: what happens to people and what happens to the land is the same thing.

Shape, I think she meant by boomerang wings, although the boomerang is something more than

that; it is something that returns. And there is great
hope in return. Not just in returned time or history,
as the round cycles of the Maya worldview express,
but in returned land and animal species. Return is
what we are banking on as we attempt to put back
what has disappeared, the songs of wolves in Yellow-
stone, the pale-edged wings of condors in California
sky, the dark, thundering herds of buffalo to Indian
country, the flamingos along the River of Hope. This
colony, once diminished to 5,000 birds in 1955, has
increased to 22,000, according to JoAnn Andrews of
Pronatura. This, and Ria Lagardos to the north, are
the only wintering and nesting areas these flamingos
have.

AND THEN WE see them, these returned flamingos, in
their wintering ground, first as a red line along the
darker water, red as volcanic fire breaking open from
black rock, revealing its passionate inner light, fire
from the center of earth's creative force, lighted from
within.

For well over a mile, all along the shore, we see
them, like dawn's red path stretched before us. It is
almost too much for the eye to see, this great vision,
the shimmering light of them. It's a vision so incredible and thick. I know it will open inside my eyes in
the moment before death when a lived life draws
itself out one last time before closing forever. We are
drawn to these birds the way air is pulled into fire.
They are proof of how far blood will travel to seek its
beginning.

We sit, floating, and watch these lives with their

grace and the black lines of their underwings. They
are noisy. The birds at the outermost edges are aware
of us. We are careful not to disturb them as they eat.
Their mission here, at the end of winter, is to fill
themselves. Already there are mating displays,
though true nesting takes place to the north of here
in Ria Lagardos, where they build and guard mud
nests.

They are restless. One group begins to fly with a
running start across water, red clouds rising across the
thin red-brown skin of water, as if water has come
undone from itself, lost something to air where
clouds, too, are born of water. Other groups are in
water and onshore, long-necked, the rose-colored
light coming from the marvelous feathers con-
structed of centuries of necessity and the love that life
has for its many forms and expressions.

They are birds glorious and godly, and like us, are
an ancient nation.

THE CLOUDS THAT were out at sea have moved east
and now they reach us. Thunder breaks open the sky
and a warm afternoon rain begins. We turn off the
engine of the boat and pole into a shadowy corridor
of mangroves until we reach a sheltered pool. A faint
wind creaks the trees. Above us, in the branches, a
termite nest is black and heavy. It is a splendid architecture wedged in the branches of a tree, one come to
over time, a creation older than human presence on
the earth by millions of years. The nest is a contained
intelligence, made up of lives that work together
with the mind of a single organism.

The word *termite* was given by Linnaeus and originally meant "end of life." That's how young and new our oldest knowledge is, because these, too, are old participants in creation, in beginnings. They break down wood, forming rich soil in a place that would otherwise be choked.

The overhead canopy of leaves shelters us. We watch the drops meet water, returning to their larger country, becoming it, re-creating it out of themselves.

This is one of the places where an underground river has broken through the shelf of limestone and risen to the surface. It is called Ojo de Agua, Eye of Water. Looking into this eye, it seems to gaze back, and in that blue gaze are tiny fish. The water is one of Earth's lanterns, the same blue of glacier light and of the Earth as seen from out in space. Beneath us, a larger fish eats algae off a fallen tree, long-legged insects move about the unclosed eye of water.

There is a second eye, and we decide to crawl through roots and dark mud to find it. Frederico, the guide, is barefoot, and barefoot is the only way to move here. As we pass through the tangles and intricacies, he offers me a hand and helps me through. His hand is strong and warm, but in spite of it, my foot slips off the convoluted roots. I think it is all right; I see the blue leaves resting on water's floor, but it is a false bottom, and my leg keeps going until both legs are in to the hip, my foot still slipping down, "To China," Frederico says as I find a limb to grasp. Here again the boundaries did not hold. What looked like bottom was merely blue leaves and algae held up by a rising current of boundless water.

And here, where the underground river ends, other beginnings are fed, other species and creations. If it were time, instead of space, scholars would call it zero date, that place where, as for the Maya, the end of one world is the beginning of another. As they interpret the world, time is alive and travels in a circle. There were other creations and worlds before the one we now inhabit; the cosmos re-forms itself.

For those who know only this one universe, to think of its origins is an overwhelming task. It means to think before time, before space, all the way back to the void that existed before creation. And for people of science, as for those of religion, the universe in its cosmic birth originated from small and minute beginnings. There was nothing and then life came into existence. Stephen Hawking says, "It was possible for the entire universe to appear out of nothing." There is a place from which all things grew into a miraculous emergence.

"All beginnings wear their endings like dark shadows," says astronomer-physicist Chet Raymo. And maybe they do. If endings are foreshadowed by their beginnings, or are in some way the same thing, it is important that we circle around and come back to look at our human myths and stories. Unlike the cyclic nature of time for the Maya, the Western tradition of beliefs within a straight line of history leads to an apocalyptic end. And stories of the end, like those of beginning, tell something about the people who created them.

In her article "What Do Stars Eat?" in *Left Bank*
Lynda Sexson writes:

> We are so accustomed to myths (sacred stories)
> of extinction, that we are not as practical at imag-
> ining that greater gap—continuation. . . . Would
> the earth or our existence on it be in such peril if
> we did not harbor a profound desire for extinc-
> tion? *"They lie down, they cannot rise, they are
> extinguished, quenched like a wick,"* resonates Isa-
> iah. The crisis of Western culture is ecological.
> The source of that crisis is in Western culture's
> own version of reality; the myth of the urge to
> eradicate: earth and images of earth, body and
> song.

Without deep reflection, we have taken on the
story of endings, assumed the story of extinction, and
have believed that it is the certain outcome of our
presence here. From this position, fear, bereavement,
and denial keep us in the state of estrangement from
our natural connection with land.

We need new stories, new terms and conditions
that are relevant to the love of land, a new narrative
that would imagine another way, to learn the infi-
nite mystery and movement at work in the world. It
would mean we, like the corn people of the Maya,
give praise and nurture creation.

Indian people must not be the only ones who
remember the agreement with the land, the sacred
pact to honor and care for the life that, in turn, pro-

vides for us. We need to reach a hand back through time and a hand forward, stand at the zero point of creation to be certain that we do not create the absence of life, of any species, no matter how inconsequential they might appear to be.

AT THE BEGINNING, there was nothing and something came from it. We have not been able to map it except in theory, in mathematical terms. As with the underground rivers, we only see where it surfaces. It is the same mystery of swimming turtles, early morning's new light, the limestone floor of sea that rose up to become land. Every piece fits and each life has its place, we learned from Darwin. As our knowledge has increased, that fitting has grown infinitely more complex and intricate. There is an integrity, a terrestrial intelligence at work. It's an intelligence far-reaching and beyond our comprehension. As Alan Lightman says: *"Creation lies outside of physics."*

The immeasurable *quality* of this world has depth and breadth we can't measure. Yet we know it's there, and we believe in it, the whole of it has been revealed only a small piece at a time. Cosmologists now surmise there are other universes. Creation is still taking place. As the story becomes larger, we become smaller. Perhaps that is why we shape belief around mystery.

WE COME FROM the land, sky, from love and the body. From matter and creation. We are, life is, an equation we cannot form or shape, a mystery we can't trace in spite of our attempts to follow it back to its origin.

As Cardenal knew by his words about the want behind our wanting, we do not even have a language to speak words deep enough, strong enough to articulate what it is we truly desire. This is just one hint of our limitations. The real alchemy of our being here is the finest of transformations, and we do not know it except to say that we are atoms that were other patterns and arrangements of form.

We do not know the secrets of stars. We do not know the true history of water. We do not know ourselves. We have forgotten that this land and every life-form is a piece of god, a divine community, with the same forces of creation in plants as in people. All the lives around us are lives of gods. The long history of creation that has shaped plankton, and shaped horseshoe crabs, has shaped our human being. Everything is Maker; mangroves, termites, all are sources of one creation or another. Without respect and reverence for it, there is an absence of holiness, of any God.

All over the earth, faces of all living things are alike.
Mother Earth has turned these faces out of the earth
with tenderness.

                                        —Luther Standing Bear

Men talk much of matter and energy, of the struggle
for existence that molds the shape of life. These things
exist, it is true; but more delicate, elusive, quicker than
fins in water, is that mysterious principle known as
organization, which leaves all other mysteries

*concerned with life stale and insignificant by
comparison. . . . Like some dark and passing shadow
within matter, it cups out the eyes' small windows or
spaces the notes of a meadow lark's song in the
interior of a mottled egg. That principle—I am
beginning to suspect—was there before the living in
the deeps of water. . . .
If "dead" water has reared up this curious landscape
. . . it must be plain even to the most devoted
materialist that the matter of which it speaks contains
amazing, if not dreadful powers, and may not
impossibly be, as Hardy has suggested, "but one mask
of many worn by the Great Face behind."*
　　　　　　　　　　—Loren Eiseley, *Night Country*

The face of the land is our face, and that of all its
creatures. To see whole is to see all the parts of the
puzzle, some of which have not even been found, as
there are still numerous animals and plants that have
not been identified. Even here at Celestun there are
faces still unseen. What grows here and what grows
within us is the same.

IN THIS PLACE are spectacular fish, deep blue ones,
green and yellow. But swimming, I see a silver circle
of fish, many small ones, swimming in a cluster. All
of them turn at one time and hold the circle together.
They avoid me, moving away, and still their circle
holds. They share a mind, the way termites do, share
a common mission of survival, like all the faces
turned out of the earth, all part of the one mask of
many worn by the Great Face behind.

The lands around my dwelling
Are more beautiful
From the day
When it is given me to see
Faces I have never seen before.
All is more beautiful.
All is more beautiful.
And life is thankfulness.
These guests of mine
Make my house grand.
                    —Eskimo song

What does god look like? These fish, this water, this land.

STORIES OF WATER

EARTH IS A WATER PLANET. IT IS A WORLD OF SALT oceans, cloud forests, underground springs, and winding rivers. It has built arches and pillars, has burrowed a deepening way into caves. It has plunged into land and been lost to other places where the long slow dripping of moisture created glittering crystals and teeth of inner earth, and as ice, it has taken the shape of large glaciers and ridden space.

The mountains where I live are young. Water still works them. With its freezing and thawing, earth gives way. Called home by gravity, slabs of stone crash heavily down to the canyon floor, and we say,

"The earth is alive, it shrugs the rocks off its tired shoulders."

In the canyon, springwater seeps out from stone walls, and we say, "Earth is weeping."

This canyon was created by a curling river that emptied itself into an inland sea a few miles down from here. The currents of that ancient sea lapped away at red stones, creating ledges and crannies that are now the nesting places of birds. It formed stone bowls that hold what is left of every rain, pools of water reflecting the face of the moon. Lizards drink there.

The same water, freezing and thawing, contracts and expands the topsoil so that earth pushes stones upward, away from gravity. In spring when we go outside, new stones are scattered here and there. We say, Land has given birth.

And it does. Everywhere water travels, life follows. In a desert, only moments after a cloudburst, the terrain quickens; a plant flowers, an insect drinks moisture from its back and survives. Frogs rise up from beneath parched earth, mate, and return again to the cool underworld.

We have ceremonies to bring rain clouds to arid lands. We sing down the rain. We smell the ceremonies of life-giving rain and hear thunder announce its presence, and the gray shafts of rain arrive from the distance. Then we celebrate the mud-filled rivers, the veins and arteries of our alive world. Seeds send forth their first shoots. Reservoirs fill, and through some amazing alchemy, water is transformed, flowing through wires into homes, light at the touch of a finger.

There are stories of magic about seas, about the dense, dangerous swamps, the peat bog that caught fire and burned for two years, even the story of science that tells how fish began a precious journey from gill slit to amphibian, learning to survive at the elemental edge between water and air before it grew wings that lifted up the blue sky.

Or, it went another way, to our own inheritance of fragile skin.

SOME YEARS AGO, I entered water's world, deep in the beautiful blue silence of the Caribbean. It was filled with slowly bending weeds and blue fish. It held me in its swaying grasp as thin yellow fish swam by. An octopus floated past like pink silk waving along a current of wind. Golden stars moved slowly, alive in caverns beside the black spines of sea urchins. I swam out farther in the cellular sea, through a school of barracuda that were all one mind, all turning at the same sharp moment. A thousand small jellyfish surrounded me in the green light of water, floating by without so much as grazing my alien skin. It was a world apart from our world. I was taken in by it, taken almost away, surfacing to find no sight of shore, no memory of how I had arrived in this suspension of life.

AS A GIRL, I went often to a small, almost invisible creek near our home to watch snails and birds that visited the water. But one year, it turned suddenly into a torrential river, roaring downhill full of stones and trees, taking earth down with it.

After the flood subsided, we looked at how earth

was changed. Around us the rust-colored earth was covered with silt and broken trees. Parts of homes rose out of mud. A roof emerged from the water-torn side of a hill. A rocking chair sat on a mound of sand. Cattle were dead and bloated, stretched out on the silted new plains of earth. A red rooster was shining like copper in a sandy knoll. We saw our once familiar world through one of nature's cold eyes. We were small. We had no choice but to bend down before water's will; it was stronger than ours.

RECENTLY, A MAN related to me his journey by canoe up the far northern waters to Hudson Bay. He and his friend, he said, had reached their destination and saw freshwater beluga whales playing beneath their canoe. Enchanted by the story, I wanted to pass through the mouth of that water in search of the white whales, wanted to see their smooth skin and limber motion, but as he talked on, the voyage he described was a crossing over of hell's river, a frightening journey of survival with mosquitoes so thick the veiled men could not open their nets even to eat, could barely see for the bloodthirsty swarms that clung to them. A single opening in a sleeve, a tear in a shirt, and they would have been overcome by the thick, hungry insects that torment caribou into their own great migrations of escape. The days were hot. The nights were freezing. In one place the water receded and left them stranded in mud. Had they arrived an hour later in that muddy mooring, they would have been unable to reach firm ground at all.

In *Call Me Ishmael*, Charles Olson writes about a

whaling quest that preceded Herman Melville's story
of the white whale, *Moby Dick*, by twenty years.
Over a year after these whalers set out to sea, their
ship was struck by a whale and sank. A week later,
those few who survived, floating in a lifeboat, made
the mistake of eating bread that had been soaked in
ocean water, and the salt of it dehydrated them, caus-
ing their skin to split and blister. The only way to
quench their thirst was to kill a turtle and drink its
blood, and occasionally a flying fish would hit the
sails of their small boat, fall inside and be swallowed
raw by the weak and hungry men:

> After a month on open sea they were glad-
> dened by the sight of a small island which they
> took to be Dulcie but was Elizabeth Isle. Currents
> and storm had taken them a thousand miles off
> their course.
> They found water on the island after a futile
> search for it from rocks which they picked at,
> where moisture was, with their hatchets. It was
> discovered in a small spring in the sand at the
> extreme verge of ebbtide. They could gather it
> only at low water. The rest of the time the sea
> flowed over the spring to the depth of six feet.

Six feet under. The depth of a man's grave. What
was it that drove them to the dead, paradoxical center
of being surrounded by water and dying of thirst?
And what was that more contemporary need for two
men from the American privileged class to pit themselves against elements at Hudson Bay, rowing to

within an inch of death's handhold? Melville himself, in spite of his writings, deserted his first whaling ship, was a mutineer on the second, and emerged mysteriously and without explanation from his third journey in Honolulu.

Perhaps they knew that water would carry them full circle face-to-face with themselves, or maybe they searched for a light stronger than that produced by barrels of sperm whale oil. The sea is a primal magnet, and maybe theirs were journeys into mystery and wilderness, a pull toward healing, toward a baptism in the enormous world of life, a coming together of land creatures with the holy waters of earth that carry not only ships and giant fish, but also our own hidden treasures. The dark inner seas seek us out like the song of ocean in a shell, and we turn back toward them, to our origins, our waters of birth.

LAST SUMMER, I traveled across Lake Superior to Isle Royale, an island most well known for its wolf and moose population. Between the mainland and the island, the boatman, who had lived in that region all his life, related this story: When he was a boy the luxury liner *The American* was shipwrecked. He watched as it disappeared beneath the water's surface. He could hear the screams of people onboard. He and his father were part of the rescue effort, helping people into lifeboats and returning them to shore. The shock of watching such a disaster caused him to lose his memory. His first recollection, a few weeks later, was of a room in his home that was filled with sweet-smelling fruit. *The American* had carried a cargo of fresh fruits, and the water of Lake Superior

was the precise temperature needed to preserve the
fruit in the hull of the capsized boat. For months
after that, divers descended into the clear blue water
and returned with red berries still intact, apples that
had been picked from mother trees and were carrying their seed, grapes and oranges, a new world, yes,
with its sweet foods, and their saved seed pods of life,
even bananas from the other America.

THE LAST TRACES of older civilizations are beneath
the water, broken down to almost nothing in the pri-
mordial oceans where mountains have become grains
of sand. Once, walking on a beach that in another life
had been the rocky terrain of dry earth, I found a
piece of smooth, gray clay. A line of sky blue glaze
crossed it, but it looked like the clay had burst open,
perhaps during firing, and in the center of that opening, a crystal was embedded. It was clear and faceted.
It appeared to have been intentionally fired inside
the clay. I treasured that tile, which I supposed to be
from the ruined, fallen world of Atlantis. It was my
share of hope that there was another, better world
than ours. Atlantis. Unlike a far heaven, unlike the
fiery, molten core of hell, Atlantis, whether it existed
or not, was a world we could believe in, a land like
our own, a society whose fruits were a new, devastat-
ing technology, a country peopled with prophets and
scientists, a world of lotus-eaters seeking beyond their
own grasp, dreaming beyond their limits, and finding their ruin within those dreams.

BUT AFTER ALL these stories, the most amazing tale
of all belongs to water's own voice, telling a story of

it's unbroken orbit from itself to itself. Between earth and earth's atmosphere, the amount of water remains constant; there is never a drop more, never a drop less. This is a story of circular infinity, of a planet birthing itself. After I learned this, the clear rain-drops began to break out of the sky, falling to ground they had passed through before. I was overwhelmed with the beauty of rain's sparkling clarity, the clear flow of it, and how any of it, in our toxic world, ever renews itself in its journey through earth and sky.

A PERSON RELATED this story to me: they were trav-eling the Amazon River, and when they rounded a bend they saw a great tree filled with enormous pink blossoms. It was vibrant and alive in the green, wet jungle. As they drew near, they were amazed to see that the branches were filled, not with flowers, but with flamingos perching in the twisted branches. It was a marvelous vision, that story from the basin filled with silver-sided fish, blue frogs, and golden cats with silent paws, that place where rain falls and rises again to the sky, turning over inside clouds, fly-ing above the emerald forests and falling.

To those of us who dwell in arid lands, this world with its bird-eating spiders, red lizards, and its immense store of fruits and nuts, seems supernatural. It carries the calling birds, the mating songs of frogs, the croaking insects. Rain's song lives there and, like everyone, I read daily that it is endangered. Half of the earth's animals live in the humid jungles, most of them yet to be named, and plants that have already transformed the history of modern, Western medicine, plants used as treatments for leukemia and Parkinson's disease. A large percentage of the Costa Rican plants are thought to contain anticancer agents, and steroids were developed from Guatemalan yams. And these forests are the place our air is born, from a marriage of water and green-leafed, dripping plants. In their verdant density, they produce over a fourth of earth's oxygen.

We are only dreamers in such abundance as could feed our hungry world. Its soil is the living tissue of our earth. It is living membrane, these rain forests carried across the globe in the shape of toothpicks and fatted cattle that will feed sharp-toothed world-eaters who have never known such richness, such fertility. Inside this place, as deforestation continues, human beings, some of them still unknown to the outside world, are also being swallowed, though the papers do not mention the human losses. Since 1900, more than half of the tribal people of Brazil have become extinct. In the past ten years alone, as the Amazon highway has been under construction, at least one new nation of people a year has been discovered.

Most of us can not imagine such worlds as are nourished and created by our planet's water, but our treasures do not exist in water, or across it, such as for the seafaring people; the treasure is water itself. It means life to us, and survival. And while water is being exiled from the land it inhabits, it has no choice but to take up residence elsewhere.

The journey of water is round, and its loss, too, moves in a circle, following us around the world as

we lose something of such immense value that we do
not yet even know its name.

OUTSIDE IT IS thawing. The creek is breaking apart.
Water seeps out of the rock canyon above me. It has
been around the world. It has lived beneath the lights
of fireflies in bayous at night when mist laid itself
about cypress trunks. It has held sea turtles in its
rocking arms. It has been the Nile River, which at
this moment is the smallest it has been in all
recorded history. It has come from the rain forest that
gave birth to our air. It brings with it the stories of
where it's been. It reminds us that we are water people. Our salt bodies, like the great round of ocean, are
pulled and held by the moon. We are creatures that
belong here. This world is in our blood and bones,
and our blood and bones are the earth.

Out from bare rock the water flows, from times
before our time. The clouds flying overhead are
rivers. Thunder breaks open, and those rivers fall,
like a sprinkling of baptismal water, giving itself
back, everything a round river, in a circle, alive and
moving.

THE KILL HOLE

I N NEW MEXICO THERE WAS AN ANCIENT PEOPLE
called the Mimbres. They were skilled potters. What
they made was far superior to the work of later potters in the Southwest. The Mimbres formed bowls
out of rich, red clay that held generations of life, and
they painted that shaped clay with animals, people,
plants, and even the dusty wind that still inhabits the
dry New Mexico land.

Like the Anasazi and other ancient nations, these
were people of the mystery, having abandoned their
place and vanished into a dimension that has
remained unknown to those of us who have come

later. But before they disappeared into the secret, the Mimbres "killed" their pots by breaking a hole in the center of each one. It is thought that the hole served to release the spirit of the pot from the clay, allowing it to travel with them over land and to join them in their burial grounds. It is called a "kill hole."

At the third death I attended, I thought of these earlier people, and wondered about the kill hole, how life escapes the broken clay of ourselves, travels away from the center of our living. It's said that at death, the fontanelle in the top of the skull opens, the way it is open when we are born into the world. Before her spirit escaped through the crown, I wanted to ask that dying woman what she could tell me about life. But dying is hard work and it leaves little time for questions. There was time only for human comfort as the woman balanced those last hours between the worlds of life and death.

That woman died in California, not far from the place where Ishi, the last Yana Indian, was found in 1911. Ishi came from a small group of Indians who lived undiscovered for over fifty years in the Mill Creek area, concealed by forest. They knew the secret of invisibility. Not even a cloud of smoke had revealed their whereabouts. But as the settling of the continent expanded to the West, and as the logging of the forests continued, Ishi was found, finally, by surveyors who must have believed he was not a man in the way they were men, for they carried away his few possessions as souvenirs for their families.

For the next four years Ishi lived in a museum as a living exhibit. He offered scholars his tools, his crafts, and his language. His was a tremendous gift to the people who were near him, but during that time he was transformed from a healthy man into a wasted skeleton. He died from tuberculosis, one of the diseases of civilization. But sometimes death has such a strange way of turning things inside out, so that what is gone becomes as important as what remains. Such an absence defines our world as surely as a Mimbres pot contains a bowl of air, or as a woman's dying body holds a memory and history of life. This is especially true in the case of Ishi; his story illuminates the world of civilization and its flaws. It tells us what kind of people we are, with our double natures. It speaks of loss and of emptiness that will never again be filled, of whole cultures disappeared, of species made extinct, all of these losses falling as if through a hole, like a spirit leaving earth's broken clay.

In our own time, there have been events as striking as the discovery of Ishi, events that, in their passing, not only raise the question of what kind of people we are, but also give us reason to ask what is our rightful place within the circle of life, we beautiful ones who are as adept at creation as we are at destruction?

ONE OF THESE events, one that haunts us like a shadow from the dark periphery of our lives, is the recent research where apes were taught American sign language. Through that language of the hands, a dialogue began between signing chimpanzees and human beings, a dialogue that bridged the species barrier. Within a relatively short time, the chimps learned to communicate with humans and with one another. They asked questions, expressed abstract thought, and combined signs and symbols to create new words they had not been taught by their human teachers. With their hands, they spoke a world of emotion, of feelings similar to our own. One angry chimp called his handler, "dirty." Another one, Ally, developed hysterical paralysis when separated from his mother. Later, one of the subjects had to be tranquilized as he was taken away, distraught and protesting, and sold into scientific research.

From these studies, we learned that primates have a capacity for love and resistance, that they not only have a rich emotional life, but that they are also able to express their pain and anguish. This is an event whose repercussions astonish us with their meaning, whose presence throws us into an identity crisis equal to that in Galileo's time when the fabric of belief was split wide open to reveal that Earth was not the center of the universe. This event bespeaks our responsibility to treat with care and tenderness all the other lives that share our small world. Yet the significance of this research has gone largely unheeded. Many members of the scientific community played down the similarities between apes and humans, ignoring the comfort of such connections. They searched instead for new definitions of language and intelligence, ones that would exclude apes from our own ways of speaking and thinking. They searched for a new division, another wall between life and life. In itself, this search sheds light on us, and in that light, we seem to have had a failure of heart.

But perhaps this armor of defense comes from another failure, from the downfall of our beliefs about who and what we are as human beings. One by one, in our lifetimes, our convictions about ourselves and our place within the world have been over-turned. Once the use of tools was considered to be strictly a human ability. Then it was found that primates and other species make use of tools. Then altruism was said to be what distinguished us from other species, until it was learned that elephants try to help their sick, staying the long hours beside their own dying ones, caressing and comforting them. And we can't even say that art is an activity that sets us apart, since those same compassionate elephants also make art. In fact, when the artist de Kooning was shown anonymous paintings by elephants, he thought the artist to be a most talented individual, one who knew how to "finish" and compose a drawing. On hearing that the artist was an elephant, he said, "That's a damned talented elephant." Jane Goodall, also on the subject of art, says that not only do chimpanzees make and name paintings, but that when shown their artwork as much as a year later, they remember the title they originally gave it.

EVEN HUMOR IS not entirely limited to humans. Recently Jane Goodall also related an exchange between the signing gorilla Koko and trainer Penny Patterson. A researcher was visiting them, and Penny wanted Koko to exhibit her intelligence. Penny held up a piece of white cloth. "Koko, what color is this?"
Koko signed, "Red."

Because the gorilla made an error, the woman asked again, "Koko, what color is this?"

Koko again replied, "Red."

Exasperated, the trainer said, "Koko, if you want to eat supper, you'd better answer the question. What color is this?"

Koko leaned forward and picked a tiny piece of red lint off the white cloth, looked her caretaker in the eye, showed her the lint, and laughed. "Red. Red, red, red!"

Still wanting a place of our own, a place set aside from the rest of the creation, now it is being ventured that maybe our ability to make fire separates us, or perhaps the desire to seek revenge. But no matter what direction the quest for separation might take, there has been a narrowing down of the difference between species, and we are forced to ask ourselves once again: what is our rightful place in the world, our responsibility to the other lives on the planet? It's a question of crucial importance as we live in this strange and confusing time, when so many of our scientists prefer to meddle with the creation of new lifeforms rather than to maintain and care for those, even human lives, who are already in our presence. Oren Lyons, Iroquois traditionalist, has said, "We forget and we consider ourselves superior, but we are after all a mere part of this creation. And we must consider to understand where we are. And we stand somewhere between the mountain and the ant, somewhere and only there as part and parcel of the creation."

We are of the animal world. We are part of the

THE KILL HOLE 115 ≡

cycles of growth and decay. Even having tried so hard
to see ourselves apart, and so often without a love for
even our own biology, we are in relationship with the
rest of the planet, and that connectedness tells us we
must reconsider the way we see ourselves and the rest
of nature.

A change is required of us, a healing of the
betrayed trust between humans and earth. Caretaking is the utmost spiritual and physical responsibility of our time, and perhaps that stewardship is
finally our place in the web of life, our work, the
solution to the mystery of what we are. There are
already so many holes in the universe that will never
again be filled, and each of them forces us to question why we permitted such loss, such tearing away
at the fabric of life, and how we will live with our
planet in the future.

Ishi is just one of those losses. Ishi was what he
called himself, and the word meant only "man." Ishi
kept his real name to himself. It was his only possession, all that remained for him of a lost way of life.
He was the last of a kind of human being. His
absence left us wondering about these lives of ours
that unfold in the center of a tragic technology.
When we wake up in the night, full of fear, we know
the hole is all around us, pulling at even our dreams.
We learn from what has fallen through before us. It's
why we study history. It's why I wished a dying
woman would balance between the worlds a
moment, teetering there, and gaze backward in time
to tell me any wise secret of survival. The kill hole

where everything falls out is not just found in earth's
or the body's clay. It is a dusky space between us and
others, the place where our compassion has fallen
away, our capacity for love failed. It is the time
between times, a breached realm where apes inform
us of a truth we fear to face. It is a broken mirror that
reveals to us our own shady and dualistic natures and
lays bare our human history of cruelty as well as love.
What we are lives in that abyss. But we have also to
ask if this research is not a great step in creating a
bridge across that broken world, if these first explo-
rations between humans and apes are not hands held
out in welcome. Some of us have reached out across
the solitude of our lives with care and mercy, have
touched away the space between us all.

There is a Mandan story that tells how the killed
buffalo left through a hole in the sky. From that hole,
it's said, the grandmother still looks down at earth,
watching over her children.

Today in San Diego, a young California condor is
breaking a hole in an egg, pecking its way through
to life. There are only twenty-eight California condors left in the world, all of them in captivity.
They've been dwelling on the brink of extinction.
But how amazing it is, this time a new life coming
in, turning another way through that hole. A mend-
ing is taking place, a life emerging like the thread
out of the labyrinth, the thread leading out of a
Navajo rug's pattern of loss. The old woman in the
sky is looking down on us, keeping watch.

DWELLINGS

Not far from where I live is a hill that was cut into by the moving water of a creek. Eroded this way, all that's left of it is a broken wall of earth that contains old roots and pebbles woven together and exposed. Seen from a distance, it is only a rise of raw earth. But up close it is something wonderful, a small cliff dwelling that looks almost as intricate and well made as those the Anasazi left behind when they vanished mysteriously centuries ago. This hill is a place that could be the starry skies of night turned inward into the thousand round holes where solitary bees have lived and died. It is a hill of tunneling rooms. At the mouths of some of the excavations, half-circles of clay beetle out like awnings shading a doorway. It is earth that was turned to clay in the mouths of the bees and spit out as they mined deeper into their dwelling places.

This place where the bees reside is at an angle safe from rain. It faces the southern sun. It is a warm and intelligent architecture of memory, learned by whatever memory lives in the blood. Many of the holes still contain the gold husks of dead bees, their faces dry and gone, their flat eyes gazing out from death's land toward the other uninhabited half of the hill that is across the creek from these catacombs.

The first time I found the residence of the bees, it was dusty summer. The sun was hot, and land was the dry color of rust. Now and then a car rumbled along the dirt road and dust rose up behind it before settling back down on older dust. In the silence, the bees made a soft droning hum. They were alive then, and working the hill, going out and returning with pollen, in and out through the holes, back and forth between daylight and the cooler, darker regions of inner earth. They were flying an invisible map through air, a map charted by landmarks, the slant of light, and a circling story they told one another about the direction of food held inside the center of yellow flowers.

SITTING IN THE hot sun, watching the small bees fly in and out around the hill, hearing the summer birds, the light breeze, I felt right in the world. I belonged there. I thought of my own dwelling places, those real and those imagined. Once I lived in a town called Manitou, which means "Great Spirit," and where hot mineral springwater gurgled beneath the streets and rose up into open wells. I felt safe there. With the underground movement of water and heat a constant reminder of other life, of what lives beneath us, it seemed to be the center of the world.

A few years after that, I wanted silence. My daydreams were full of places I longed to be, shelters and solitudes. I wanted a room apart from others, a hidden cabin to rest in. I wanted to be in a redwood forest with trees so tall the owls called out in the daytime. I daydreamed of living in a vapor cave a few hours away from here. Underground, warm, and moist, I thought it would be the perfect world for staying out of cold winter, for escaping the noise of living.

And how often I've wanted to escape to a wilderness where a human hand has not been in everything. But those were only dreams of peace, of comfort, of a nest inside stone or woods, a sanctuary where a dream or life wouldn't be invaded.

YEARS AGO, IN the next canyon west of here, there was a man who followed one of those dreams and moved into a cave that could only be reached by climbing down a rope. For years he lived there in comfort, like a troglodite. The inner weather was stable, never too hot, too cold, too wet, or too dry. But then he felt lonely. His utopia needed a woman. He went to town until he found a wife. For a while after the marriage, his wife climbed down the rope along with him, but before long she didn't want the mice scurrying about in the cave, or the untidy bats that wanted to hang from stones of the ceiling. So they built a door. Because of the closed entryway, the temperature changed. They had to put in heat. Then the inner moisture of earth warped the door, so they had to have air-conditioning, and after that the earth wanted to go about life in its own way and it didn't give in to the people.

IN OTHER DAYS and places, people paid more attention to the strong-headed will of earth. Once homes were built of wood that had been felled from a single region in a forest. That way, it was thought, the house would hold together more harmoniously, and the family of walls would not fall or lend themselves to the unhappiness or arguments of the inhabitants.

AN ITALIAN IMMIGRANT to Chicago, Aldo Piacenzi, built birdhouses that were dwellings of harmony and peace. They were the incredible spired shapes of cathedrals in Italy. They housed not only the birds, but also his memories, his own past. He painted them the watery blue of his Mediterranean, the wild rose of flowers in a summer field. Inside them was straw and the droppings of lives that layed eggs, fledglings who grew there. What places to inhabit, the bright and sunny birdhouses in dreary alleyways of the city.

ONE BEAUTIFUL AFTERNOON, cool and moist, with the kind of yellow light that falls on earth in these arid regions, I waited for barn swallows to return from

their daily work of food gathering. Inside the tunnel
where they live, hundreds of swallows had mixed
their saliva with mud and clay, much like the solitary bees, and formed nests that were perfect as a pot-
ter's bowl. At five in the evening, they returned all
at once, a dark, flying shadow. Despite their enormous numbers and the crowding together of nests,
they didn't pause for even a moment before entering
the nests, nor did they crowd one another. Instantly
they vanished into the nests. The tunnel went silent.
It held no outward signs of life.

But I knew they were there, filled with the fire of
living. And what a marriage of elements was in those
nests. Not only mud's earth and water, the fire of sun
and dry air, but even the elements contained one
another. The bodies of prophets and crazy men were
broken down in that soil.

I'VE NOTICED OFTEN how when a house is abandoned,
it begins to sag. Without a tenant, it has no need to
go on. If it were a person, we'd say it is depressed or
lonely. The roof settles in, the paint cracks, the walls
and floorboards warp and slope downward in their
own natural ways, telling us that life must stay in
everything as the world whirls and tilts and moves
through boundless space.

ONE SUMMER DAY, cleaning up after long-eared owls
where I work at a rehabilitation facility for birds of
prey, I was raking the gravel floor of a flight cage.
Down on the ground, something looked like it was
moving. I bent over to look into the pile of bones and

pellets I'd just raked together. There, close to the
ground, were two fetal mice. They were new to the
planet, pink and hairless. They were so tenderly
young. Their faces had swollen blue-veined eyes.
They were nestled in a mound of feathers, soft as vel-
vet, each one curled up smaller than an infant's ear,
listening to the first sounds of earth. But the ants
were biting them. They turned in agony, unable to
pull away, not yet having the arms or legs to move,
but feeling, twisting away from, the pain of the bites.
I was horrified to see them bitten out of life that way.
I dipped them in water, as if to take away the sting,
and let the ants fall in the bucket. Then I held the
tiny mice in the palm of my hand. Some of the ants
were drowning in the water. I was trading one life
for another, exchanging the lives of ants for those of
mice, but I hated their suffering, and hated even
more that they had not yet grown to a life, and
already they inhabited the miserable world of pain.
Death and life feed each other. I know that.

Inside these rooms where birds are healed, there
are other lives besides those of mice. There are fine
gray globes the wasps have woven together, the
white cocoons of spiders in a corner, the downward
tunneling anthills. All these dwellings are inside one
small walled space, but I think most about the mice.
Sometimes the downy nests fall out of the walls
where their mothers have placed them out of the way
of their enemies. When one of the nests falls, they
are so well made and soft, woven mostly from the
chest feathers of birds. Sometimes the leg of a small
quail holds the nest together like a slender corner-

stone with dry, bent claws. The mice have adapted to
life in the presence of their enemies, adapted to living in the thin wall between beak and beak, claw and
claw. They move their nests often, as if a new rafter
or wall will protect them from the inevitable fate of
all our returns home to the deeper, wider nest of
earth that houses us all.

ONE AUGUST AT Zia Pueblo during the corn dance I
noticed tourists picking up shards of all the old pot-
tery that had been made and broken there. The residents of Zia know not to take the bowls and pots left
behind by the older ones. They know that the fragments of those earlier lives need to be smoothed back
to earth, but younger nations, travelers from continents across the world who have come to inhabit this
land, have little of their own to grow on. The pieces
of earth that were formed into bowls, even on their
way home to dust, provide the new people a lifeline
to an unknown land, help them remember that they
live in the old nest of earth.

IT WAS IN early February, during the mating season
of the great horned owls. It was dusk, and I hiked up
the back of a mountain to where I'd heard the owls a
year before. I wanted to hear them again, the voices
so tender, so deep, like a memory of comfort. I was
halfway up the trail when I found a soft, round nest.
It had fallen from one of the bare-branched trees. It
was a delicate nest, woven together of feathers, sage,
and strands of wild grass. Holding it in my hand in
the rosy twilight, I noticed that a blue thread was

entwined with the other gatherings there. I pulled at the thread a little, and then I recognized it. It was a thread from one of my skirts. It was blue cotton. It was the unmistakable color and shape of a pattern I knew. I liked it, that a thread of my life was in an abandoned nest, one that had held eggs and new life. I took the nest home. At home, I held it to the light and looked more closely. There, to my surprise, nestled into the gray-green sage, was a gnarl of black hair. It was also unmistakable. It was my daughter's hair, cleaned from a brush and picked up out in the sun beneath the maple tree, or the pit cherry where birds eat from the overladen, fertile branches until only the seeds remain on the trees.

I didn't know what kind of nest it was, or who had lived there. It didn't matter. I thought of the remnants of our lives carried up the hill that way and turned into shelter. That night, resting inside the walls of our home, the world outside weighed so heavily against the thin wood of the house. The sloped roof was the only thing between us and the universe. Everything outside of our wooden boundaries seemed so large. Filled with night's citizens, it all came alive. The world opened in the thickets of the dark. The wild grapes would soon ripen on the vines. The burrowing ones were emerging. Horned owls sat in treetops. Mice scurried here and there. Skunks, fox, the slow and holy porcupine, all were passing by this way. The young of the solitary bees were feeding on pollen in the dark. The whole world was a nest on its humble tilt, in the maze of the universe, holding us.

THE VOYAGERS

I REMEMBER ONE NIGHT, LYING ON THE MOIST SPRING earth beside my mother. The fire of stars stretched away from us, and the mysterious darkness traveled without limit beyond where we lay on the turning earth. I could smell the damp new grass that night, but I could not touch or hold such black immensity that lived above our world, could not contain within myself even a small corner of the universe.

There seemed to be two kinds of people; earth people and those others, the sky people, who stumbled over pebbles while they walked around with their heads in clouds. Sky people loved different worlds than I loved; they looked at nests in treetops and followed the long white snake of vapor trails. But I was an earth person, and while I loved to gaze up at night and stars, I investigated the treasures at my feet, the veined wing of a dragonfly opening a delicate blue window to secrets of earth, a lusterless beetle that drank water thirstily from the tip of my finger and was transformed into sudden green and metallic brilliance. It was enough mystery for me to ponder the bones inside our human flesh, bones that through some incredible blueprint of life grow from a moment's sexual passion between a woman and a man, walk upright a short while, then walk themselves back to dust.

Years later, lost in the woods one New Year's eve, a friend found the way home by following the north star, and I began to think that learning the sky might be a practical thing. But it was the image of earth from out in space that gave me upward-gazing eyes. It was that same image that gave the sky people an anchor in the world, for it returned us to our planet in a new and loving way.

To dream of the universe is to know that we are small and brief as insects, born in a flash of rain and gone a moment later. We are delicate and our world is fragile. It was the transgression of Galileo to tell us that we were not the center of the universe, and now, even in our own time, the news of our small being here is treacherous enough that early in the space program, the photographs of Earth were classified as secret documents by the government. It was thought, and rightfully so, that the image of our small blue

Earth would forever change how we see ourselves in context with the world we inhabit.

When we saw the deep blue and swirling white turbulence of our Earth reflected back to us, says photographer Steven Meyers, we also saw "the visual evidence of creative and destructive forces moving around its surface, we saw for the first time the deep blackness of that which surrounds it, we sensed directly, and probably for the first time, our incredibly profound isolation, and the special fact of our being here." It was a world whose intricately linked-together ecosystem could not survive the continuing blows of exploitation.

In 1977, when the Voyagers were launched, one of these spacecraft carried the Interstellar Record, a hoped-for link between earth and space that is filled with the sounds and images of the world around us. It carries parts of our lives all the way out to the great Forever. It is destined to travel out of our vast solar system, out to the far, unexplored regions of space in hopes that somewhere, millions of years from now, someone will find it like a note sealed in a bottle carrying our history across the black ocean of space. This message is intended for the year 8,000,000.

One greeting onboard from Western India says: "Greetings from a human being of the Earth. Please contact." Another, from Eastern China, but resembling one that could have been sent by my own Chickasaw people, says: "Friends of space, how are you all? Have you eaten yet? Come visit us if you have time."

There is so much hope in those greetings, such

sweetness. If found, these messages will play our world to a world that's far away. They will sing out the strangely beautiful sounds of Earth, sounds that in all likelihood exist on no other planet in the universe. By the time the record is found, if ever, it is probable that the trumpeting bellows of elephants, the peaceful chirping of frogs and crickets, the wild dogs baying out from the golden needle and record, will be nothing more than a gone history of what once lived on this tiny planet in the curving tail of a spiral galaxy. The undeciphered language of whales will speak to a world not our own, to people who are not us. They will speak of what we value the most on our planet, things that in reality we are almost missing.

A small and perfect world is traveling there, with psalms journeying past Saturn's icy rings, all our treasured life flying through darkness, going its way alone back through the universe. There is the recorded snapping of fire, the song of a river traveling the continent, the living wind passing through dry grasses, all the world that burns and pulses around us, even the comforting sound of a heartbeat taking us back to the first red house of our mothers' bodies, all that, floating through the universe.

The Voyager carries music. A Peruvian wedding song is waiting to be heard in the far, distant regions of space. The Navajo Night Chant travels through darkness like medicine for healing another broken world. Blind Willie Johnson's slide guitar and deep down blues are on that record, in night's long territory.

The visual records aboard the Voyager depict a
nearly perfect world, showing us our place within the
whole; in the image of a snow-covered forest, trees
are so large that human figures standing at their base
are almost invisible. In the corner of this image is a
close-up of a snow crystal's elegant architecture of ice
and air. Long-necked geese fly across another picture,
a soaring eagle. Three dolphins, sun bright on their
silver sides, leap from a great ocean wave. Beneath
them are underwater blue reefs with a shimmering
school of fish. It is an abundant, peaceful world, one
where a man eats from a vine heavy with grapes, an
old man walks through a field of white daisies, and
children lovingly touch a globe in a classroom. To
think that the precious images of what lives on earth
beside us, the lives we share with earth, some endangered, are now tumbling through time and space,
more permanent than we are, and speaking the
sacred language of life that we ourselves have only
just begun to remember.

We have sent a message that states what we most
value here on earth; respect for all life and ways. It
is a sealed world, a seed of what we may become.
What an amazing document is flying above the
clouds, holding Utopia. It is more magical and heavy
with meaning than the cave paintings of Lascaux,
more wise than the language of any holy book. These
are images that could sustain us through any cold
season of ice or hatred or pain.

In *Murmurs of Earth*, written by members of the
committee who selected the images and recordings,
the records themselves are described in a way that

attests to their luminous quality of being: "They glis-
ten, golden, in the sunlight, . . . encased in aluminum
cocoons." It sounds as though, through some magical
metamorphosis, this chrysalis of life will emerge in
another part of infinity, will grow to a wholeness of
its own, and return to us alive, full-winged, red, and
brilliant.

There is so much hope there that it takes us away
from the dark times of horror we live in, a time when
the most cruel aspects of our natures have been
revealed to us in regions of earth named Auschwitz,
Hiroshima, My Lai, and Rwanda, a time when tele-
vised death is the primary amusement of our children, when our children are killing one another on
the streets.

At second glance, this vision for a new civilization,
by its very presence, shows us what is wrong with our
world. Defining Utopia, we see what we could be
now, on earth, at this time, and next to the images of
a better world, that which is absent begins to cry out.
The underside of our lives grows in proportion to
what is denied. The darkness is made darker by the
record of light. A screaming silence falls between the
stars of space. Held inside that silence are the sounds
of gunfire, the wailings of grief and hunger, the last,
extinct song of a bird. The dammed river goes dry,
along with its valleys. Illnesses that plague our bodies
live in this crack of absence. The broken link
between us and the rest of our world grows too large,
and the material of nightmares grows deeper while
the promises for peace and equality are empty, are
merely dreams without reality.

But how we want it, how we want that half-faced, one-sided God.

In earlier American days, when Catholic missions were being erected in Indian country, a European woman, who was one of the first white contacts for a northern tribe of people, showed sacred paintings to an Indian woman. The darker woman smiled when she saw a picture of Jesus and Mary encircled in their haloes of light. A picture of the three kings with their crowns and gifts held her interest. But when she saw a picture of the crucifixion, the Indian woman hurried away to warn others that these were dangerous people, people to fear, who did horrible things to one another. This picture is not carried by the Voyager, for fear we earth people would "look" cruel. There is no image of this man nailed to a cross, no saving violence. There are no political messages, no photographs of Hiroshima. This is to say that we know our own wrongdoings.

Nor is there a true biology of our species onboard because NASA officials vetoed the picture of a naked man and pregnant woman standing side by side, calling it "smut." They allowed only silhouettes to be sent, as if our own origins, the divine flux of creation that passes between a man and a woman, are unacceptable, something to hide. Even picture diagrams of the human organs, musculature, and skeletal system depict no sexual organs, and a photograph showing the birth of an infant portrays only the masked, gloved physician lifting the new life from a mass of sheets, the mother's body hidden. While we might ask if they could not have sent the carved stone gods and goddesses in acts of beautiful sexual intimacy on temple walls in India, this embarrassment about our own carriage of life and act of creative generation nevertheless reveals our feelings of physical vulnerability and discomfort with our own life force.

From an American Indian perspective, there are other problems here. Even the language used in the selection process bespeaks many of the failings of an entire system of thought and education. From this record, we learn about our relationships, not only with people, but with everything on earth. For example, a small gold-eyed frog seen in a human hand might have been a photograph that bridges species, a statement of our kinship with other lives on earth, but the hand is described, almost apologetically, as having "a dirty fingernail." Even the clay of creation has ceased to be the rich element from which life grows. I recall that the Chilean poet Pablo Neruda wrote "What can I say without touching the earth with my hands?" We must wonder what of value can ever be spoken from lives that are lived outside of life, without a love or respect for the land and other lives.

In *Murmurs of Earth*, one of the coauthors writes about hearing dolphins from his room, "breathing, playing with one another. Somehow," he says, "one had the feeling that they weren't just some sea creatures but some very witty and intelligent beings living in the next room." This revealing choice of words places us above and beyond the rest of the world, as though we have stepped out of our natural cycles in our very existence here on earth. And isn't our world full of those rooms? We inhabit only a small space in the house of life. In another is a field of corn. In one more is the jungle world of the macaw. Down the hall, a zebra is moving. Beneath the foundation is the world of snakes and the five beating hearts of the earthworm.

In so many ways, the underside of our lives is here. Even the metals used in the record tell a story about the spoils of inner earth, the laborers in the hot mines. Their sweat is in that record, hurtling away from our own galaxy.

What are the possibilities, we wonder, that our time capsule will be found? What is the possibility that there are lives other than our own in the universe? Our small galaxy, the way of the milk, the way of sustenance, is only one of billions of galaxies, but there is also the possibility that we are the only planet where life opens, blooms, is gone, and then turns over again. We hope this is not the case. We are so young we hardly know what it means to be a human being, to have natures that allow for war. We barely even know our human histories, so much having unraveled before our time, and while we know that our history creates us, we hope there is another place, another world we can fly to when ours is running out. We have come so far away from wisdom, a wisdom that is the heritage of all people, an old kind of knowing that respects a community of land, animals, plants, and other people as equal to ourselves. Where we know the meaning of relationship.

As individuals, we are not faring much better. We are young. We hardly know who we are. We face the search for ourselves alone. In spite of our search through the universe, we do not know our own personal journeys. We still wonder if the soul weighs half an ounce, if it goes into the sky at the time of our death, if it also reaches out, turning, through the universe.

But still, this innocent reaching out is a form of ceremony, as if the Voyager were a sacred space, a ritual enclosure that contains our dreaming the way a cathedral holds the bones of saints.

The people of earth are reaching out. We are having a collective vision. Like young women and men on a vision quest, we seek a way to live out the peace of the vision we have sent to the world of stars. We want to live as if there is no other place, as if we will always be here. We want to live with devotion to the world of waters and the universe of life that dwells above our thin roofs.

I remember that night with my mother, looking up at the black sky with its turning stars. It was a mystery, beautiful and distant. Her body I came from, but our common ancestor is the earth, and the ancestor of earth is space. That night we were small, my mother and I, and we were innocent. We were children of the universe. In the gas and dust of life, we are voyagers. Wait. Stop here a moment. Have you eaten? Come in. Eat.

THE SNAKE PEOPLE

ONE GREEN AND HUMID SUMMER, MY FATHER AND I
were driving through the hot Oklahoma countryside.
I had just handed over the wheel of the truck to him
and was bathing my face with a wet cloth when
something that looked like a long golden strand of
light leapt up, twisted in the wavering air, and flew
lightning fast across the road. We stopped, both of us
jumping out, in time to see the golden racer vanish
into the kingdom of roots and soil.

That flying snake, that thin flash of light, brought
back a store of memories. Our lives have been peopled with snakes and stories of snakes: there was my

Chickasaw grandfather who, riding his stocky, thick-muscled horse, could smell the reptile odor from a distance, and thus keep his horses away from rattlers curled beneath rocks or stretched out in the warm sun. And my Aunt Louise had a reputation for swimming among water mocassins so smoothly that they did not take note of her. Then there was the time my father and I were digging for fishing worms when we came across an abandoned well.

The well was in the middle of a dry Oklahoma emptiness, where that year's summer heat had cracked earth into broken tiles of red clay. The well was covered with a plank of wood, a heavy stone placed on top to hold it down in windstorms and to keep children my size from falling in. We moved the stone, lifted the wooden lid, and peered down into the cool, dark cistern. It smelled dank and rich, a welcome moisture in the hot summer. It was lined with round stones all the way down the musty darkness. Inside, not far from the surface of ground and raising itself out from the stones, a blue racer was gliding into the newly lighted air, its tongue calculating the world. Quickly, my father caught it. He held it just behind the head for a while, then put it in my hands, and when we returned to my grandmother's house that day, I was happy thinking of what a big fish we would catch with it. I remember still the grayish blue color of it, like a heron, the slenderness, and the dry beauty that wound down toward the dusty ground, wanting to escape me.

There were other stories, those in which snakes were fearsome creatures; a rattlesnake curled up around a telephone, ready to strike an answering hand, a snake in a swamp cooler, or crawled into bed with one of the children. And there was the time my brother woke to feel the weight of a rattlesnake heavy between his knees.

Most of the snakes of my childhood, even those without venom, were greeted by death held in human hands. They were killed with shovels, hoes, sticks, and sometimes with guns. Most people are uneasy about sharing territory with snakes. Last year, hearing a gunshot, I went up the road to see what had happened. A neighbor, shaken, told me that he had just killed a rattlesnake. He'd heard it, he said, on his front porch. At first he thought it was some kind of a motor running, but then he spotted the snake curled up there, and he stole away in search of his rifle. And this year, a seven-foot bull snake, not dangerous, was killed by another neighbor. The snake was dead. Its vulnerable, turned-up stomach was metallic and yellow, the red wounds visible. This neighbor, a tough-looking Harley biker in black leather, watched the dead snake nervously, as if it might, at any moment, return to life.

Looking back on the blue racer of Oklahoma, that thin pipe of life, I believe that snake, too, must have met with its death in our discovery of it. But its graceful life, not its death, is what has remained in my memory. And down through the years, I have come to love the snakes and their long, many-ribbed bodies.

My love was strengthened years ago when I dreamed of a woman who placed a fantastic snake

over her face. The snake was green and the woman
merged with it, wearing it like a mask, her teeth fitting inside its fangs, her face inside its green
beaklike, smooth-scaled face. They became one. Her
breath became the snake's slow breathing, and they
lived through one another, inhabiting a tropical
world of wet leaves, vines, and heavy, perfumed
flowers. As the woman began to dance, other people
emerged from the forest wearing feathers, deep blue
and emerald green, like human birds brilliant with
the dew on them. They joined the snake woman in a
dance, placing their hands on one another's waists
the way Chickasaws, my tribe, sometimes dance.
Everything became alive with the movement of that
dance. But after a while, the music became sadder
than the jungle, and both disappeared a bit at a time
behind the large dark leaves, vanishing behind rain
into the rich, fertile song of water. The woman
removed the snake and placed it on a wall where it
hung alive and beautiful, waiting for another ceremonial dance. The woman said, "All the people have
pieces of its skin. If they save the pieces, it will
remain alive. If everyone owns it, it will be preserved."

At first I thought this dream was about Indian tradition, how if each person retains part of a history,
an entire culture and lifeway remains intact and
alive, one thing living through the other, as the
snake and woman in the dream. But since that time,
I've expanded my vision. Now, it seems that what
needs to be saved, even in its broken pieces, is earth
itself, the tradition of life, the beautiful blue-green

world that lives in the coiling snake of the Milky Way.

IT IS LATE spring. Pollen is floating in the air. I am walking up the road when I see an incredible sight. A snake, four feet long, is stretched out straight as a stick across the road. It sees me coming, or I should say feels me, my feet on the ground, and without winding or curving it moves slowly off the road, remaining straight as the shadow of a fence post. It moves off the road so carefully and mysteriously, an inch at a time, as though it is sliding off ice. It disappears into the bushes, and by the time I reach the place, there is no trace that it had been there. But I stand and listen for it, because a friend who once kept snakes for milking venom told me he located snakes by the whispering sound made as they brushed through the grasses.

He once saw a black racer carried into the sky by a red-tailed hawk. It was alive and whipping through air as it tried to get loose from the sharp claws that held it, when another hawk appeared and fought to take the snake from the claws of the first. Fighting with beak and claws, the birds became involved in their hunger struggle, but as they fought, the snake came loose and began a steep descent to earth. Seeing it, both hawks forgot their fight and dove straight down after it, but the snake, still twisting, landed in a thick canopy of trees where it may have found shelter and survived.

I once saw an eagle carrying a snake through the sky to its nest. I wouldn't have noticed it if not for

my dog, Annie, who stopped in the road, staring
upward with something like awe and surprise in her
face. Birds of prey, like those hawks and that eagle,
are natural enemies of snakes and can sight them
from far off. But another time, I saw a snake swallowing a bird, the twiglike feet sticking out of the
snake's wide mouth.

AT FLOOD TIME, the vulnerable snakes emerge from
rocky ground and move upward, to hills and mounds,
seeking refuge from the torrential waters that invade
their homes. Silver with water, they wind about one
another, slide over stones and through mud, and then
rise up the rough trunks of trees where they wrap
themselves around branches and wait out the storm.
Gold-eyed, they stretch across the limbs, some loop-
ing down, some curled tight and nestlike between
branch and trunk, their double tongues darting out
like weather vanes. They remind me of women who
know they are beautiful.

BEFORE SNAKE BECAME the dark god of our underworld, burdened with human sin, it carried a different weight in our human bones; it was a being of
holy inner earth. The smooth gold eye, the hundred
ribs holding life, it coiled beautifully and mysteriously around the world of human imagination. In
nearly all ancient cultures the snake was the symbol
of healing and wholeness. Even the old ones, like the
Adena people, who left no recorded history, left a
tribute to the snake in one of the mounds near Chill-
icothe, Ohio. Over 1,200 feet in length, the mound is

an earth sculpture of an open-mouthed serpent that clasps an egg, a new potential for life, between its jaws. This is only one of many worldwide images of snakes, some curled about an egg, others with tail in mouth, telling us about the germinal beginnings of life and renewal, of infinity gone in a circle round itself.

In more recent times, the snake has symbolized our wrongs, our eating from the tree of knowledge, our search and desire for the dangerous revelations of life's mystery. In only a short duration of time in earth's history, the power of that search, the drive toward knowledge, has brought ruin to our Eden. Knowledge without wisdom, compassion, or understanding has damned us as we have been stirring about in the origins of life, breaking apart the miniature worlds of atoms just to see where that breaking will take us.

EVERY YEAR THE Hopi, whose name means "People of Peace," participate in a snake dance. They have a strong understanding of the snake people who have lived in the land long before humans were here. Snakes are the old ones, immortals who shed a milky skin to reveal the new and shining. For as long as anyone remembers, the cared-for snakes have been fed with pollen, stroked with feathers, placed on a circle of finely ground meal, and then carried into the dance. Afterward, they are returned unharmed to the thick dry dust and heat of the red land, to the dens they have lived inside for many thousands and thousands of generations. Writer Frank Waters has noted it is the oldest ceremony and ritual in the history of our continent, and it is danced by some of the oldest people who have continuously inhabited and grown from this holy land.

EVEN FURTHER BACK than those people of peace, or deeper, I should say, the image of snakes twined about a tree or one another looks surprisingly like the double, twisted helix of DNA, the spiral arrangement of molecules that we share with every other living thing on earth, plant and animal, down to the basic stuff of ourselves. Perhaps Snake dwells at the zero of ourselves, takes us full circle in a return to the oldest knowledge, which says that the earth is alive. Our bodies, if not our minds, know that zero, that core, the constellation of life at our human beginnings, that same shape of the galaxy.

I CALL THEM people. That's what they are. They have been here inhabiting the same dens for tens of thousands of generations, threading between rocks, stretching in the sun, disappearing into the grass. They belong here. They love their freedom, their dwelling places, and often die of sadness when kept in captivity.

I AM WALKING on the red road when I see the silver snake. It has been hit by a car and is dying, writhing in the place where it has only a moment earlier been full of life and stretched out on the warm, sunny road. Looking close, I notice the slit in the snake's slender belly, a gaping wound. By now the snake is dead. An infant snake is hanging out from that wound. At first I think it is an unborn snake not yet come to life in the world. I am calculating the kind of food I will need for an infant snake when it comes to me that this snake lays eggs and that this smaller one is not waiting to be born, but has been swallowed. Looking closer, I see another fall out the thin sleeve of snake. Still another falls from the dry scales. I tug at it, and several more spill out. It is strange to see them open out that way, as if blooming from the skinny tunnel of what had been alive just a few moments ago. Then—surprise—I see one of them move. It is alive, freed of its prison, somehow surviving. It must not yet have passed from the gullet into the stomach's strong digestive fluids. The tiny snake darts away and vanishes into stones and grass. It leaves a winding, thin path in the road dust. Maybe it is writing a story of survival there on the road, of what is left of wilderness, or of what has become of earth's lesser gods as one by one they disappear.

PORCUPINE

FOR YEARS, I'VE SEEN THE DARK OLD PORCUPINE LUM-
bering like a sleepwalker along the edge of the dirt
road. Late at night, she steps aside from car lights and
from the cloudy dust of tires.

This is not the porcupine of poems, the one that
eats the hand-salted shovel handle and is killed
because it desires to swallow what men have touched
with their working hands. It is not one of the sleek
young porcupines I have seen in the tops of winter
trees, silent, their dark eyes looking down over the
cold white forests, nor is it one of the fast ones who
leave their quills in the muzzles of dogs.

This one is torn and lame and her undignified quills are broken on one side, as if she has slept them tangled. She hobbles and limps away from her many batterings. She wears her history, dark and spiney, and there is a light in her, a fire around the dreary sharp halo of quills.

She has grown and walks and lives and continues, red blood pulsing through her heart and arteries, the red muscle lying over and upon itself, the organs so perfect inside, the air passing in and out as she breathes.

The black claws of her feet are like lacquer. This is the porcupine of the dirt road, the porcupine of the cattle fences, the animal of dark nights where I would see her from the shadowy corner of my eye.

One evening I find her lying dead beside the road. She has come closer to the houses than usual. The thick hairs are visible among the broken quills. I look closely at her, the clean long gaze that death permits us. Her face is sweet and dark, her inner light replaced by the light of sky. The drifting clouds are in her eyes.

As for me, I have a choice between honoring that dark life I've seen so many years moving in the junipers, or of walking away and going on with my own human busyness. There is always that choice for humans.

I lean over and pick sage and offer it to this animal old woman who lived on earth, who breathed the same air that for years I have been breathing, and that breath prays for all creatures on earth. I remove some quills. I prick my fingers several times, bent there in the dust pulling the sharpness out of death.

By the next morning the porcupine is already sagging. She is nothing but bony angles beneath fur and quill. Her face is gone, and suddenly I notice that the road is alive. Yes, it is moving and alive, and the motion of it surprises me. I turn to look, and the road is full of thousands of fat white maggots. They are leaving the porcupine. The road is an ocean of white. It has a current. Some of the maggots are turning to beetles and flies before they even reach the other side of the road. A wing breaks through here, a black leg there. They lose their white skin, and in their first changing of life, they are crossing the road and are being eaten on the other side by ants that are waiting there.

In that crossing over, that swallowing, the battle of life with life, the porcupine lives on. It lives on in the buzzing of flies and the ants with their organized lives. In its transformation, life continues. My life too, which stopped only for a small moment in history, in the great turning over of the world.

WAKING UP THE RAKE

IN THE STILL DARK MORNINGS, MY GRANDMOTHER would rise up from her bed and put wood in the stove. When the fire began to burn, she would sit in front of its warmth and let down her hair. It had never been cut, and it knotted down in two long braids. When I was fortunate enough to be there, in those red Oklahoma mornings, I would wake up with her, stand behind her chair, and pull the brush through the long strands of her hair. It cascaded down her back, down over the chair, and touched the floor.

We were the old and the new, bound together in

front of the snapping fire, woven like a lifetime's tangled growth of hair. I saw my future in her body and face, and her past was alive in me. We were morning people, and in all of earth's mornings the new intertwines with the old. Even new, a day itself is ancient, old with earth's habit of turning over and over again.

Years later, I was sick, and I went to a traditional healer. The healer was dark and thin and radiant. The first night I was there, she also lit a fire. We sat before it, smelling the juniper smoke. She asked me to tell her everything, my life spoken in words, a case history of living, with its dreams and losses, the scars and wounds we all bear from being in the world. She smoked me with cedar smoke, wrapped a sheet around me, and put me to bed, gently, like a mother caring for her child.

The next morning she nudged me awake and took me outside to pray. We faced east, where the sun was beginning its journey on our side of earth.

The following morning in red dawn, we went outside and prayed. The sun was a full orange eye rising up the air. The morning after that we did the same, and on Sunday we did likewise.

The next time I visited her it was a year later, and again we went through the same prayers, standing outside facing the early sun. On the last morning I was there, she left for her job in town. Before leaving, she said, "Our work is our altar."

Those words have remained with me.

Now I am a disciple of birds. The birds that I mean are eagles, owls, and hawks. I clean cages at the Birds of Prey Rehabilitation Foundation. It is the work I wanted to do, in order to spend time inside the gentle presence of birds.

There is a Sufi saying that goes something like this: "Yes, worship God, go to church, sing praises, but first tie your camel to the post." This cleaning is the work of tying the camel to a post.

I pick up the carcasses and skin of rats, mice, and of rabbits. Some of them have been turned inside out by the sharp-beaked eaters, so that the leathery flesh becomes a delicately veined coat for the inner fur. It is a boneyard. I rake the smooth fragments of bones. Sometimes there is a leg or shank of deer to be picked up.

In this boneyard, the still-red vertebrae lie on the ground beside an open rib cage. The remains of a rabbit, a small intestinal casing, holds excrement like beads in a necklace. And there are the clean, oval pellets the birds spit out, filled with fur, bone fragments, and now and then, a delicate sharp claw that looks as if it were woven inside. A feather, light and soft, floats down a current of air, and it is also picked up.

Over time, the narrow human perspective from which we view things expands. A deer carcass begins to look beautiful and rich in its torn redness, the muscle and bone exposed in the shape life took on for a while as it walked through meadows and drank at creeks.

And the bone fragments have their own stark beauty, the clean white jawbones with ivory teeth small as the head of a pin still in them. I think of medieval physicians trying to learn about our private, hidden bodies by cutting open the stolen dead and finding the splendor inside, the grace of every red organ, and the smooth, gleaming bone.

This work is an apprenticeship, and the birds are the teachers. Sweet-eyed barn owls, such taskmasters, asking us to be still and slow and to move in time with their rhythms, not our own. The short-eared owls with their startling yellow eyes require the full presence of a human. The marsh hawks behind their branches watch our every move.

There is a silence needed here before a person enters the bordered world the birds inhabit, so we stop and compose ourselves before entering their doors, and we listen to the musical calls of the eagles, the sound of wings in air, the way their feet with sharp black claws, many larger than our own hands, grab hold of a perch. Then we know we are ready to enter, and they are ready for us.

The most difficult task the birds demand is that we learn to be equal to them, to feel our way into an intelligence that is different from our own. A friend, awed at the thought of working with eagles, said, "Imagine knowing an eagle." I answered her honestly, "It isn't so much that we know the eagles. It's that they know us."

And they know that we are apart from them, that as humans we have somehow fallen from our animal grace, and because of that we maintain a distance from them, though it is not always a distance of heart. The places we inhabit, even sharing a common earth, must remain distinct and separate. It was our presence that brought most of them here in the first place, nearly all of them injured in a clash with the human world. They have been shot, or hit by cars, trapped in leghold traps, poisoned, ensnared in wire fences. To ensure their survival, they must remember us as the enemies that we are. We are the embodiment of a paradox; we are the wounders and we are the healers.

There are human lessons to be learned here, in the work. Fritjof Capra wrote: "Doing work that has to be done over and over again helps us recognize the natural cycles of growth and decay, of birth and death, and thus become aware of the dynamic order of the universe." And it is true, in whatever we do, the brushing of hair, the cleaning of cages, we begin to see the larger order of things. In this place, there is a constant coming to terms with both the sacred place life occupies, and with death. Like one of those early physicians who discovered the strange, inner secrets of our human bodies, I'm filled with awe at the very presence of life, not just the birds, but a horse contained in its living fur, a dog alive and running. What a marvel it is, the fine shape life takes in all of us. It is equally marvelous that life is quickly turned back to earth-colored ants and the soft white maggots that are time's best and closest companions. To sit with the eagles and their flutelike songs, listening to the longer flute of wind sweep through the lush grasslands, is to begin to know the natural laws that exist apart from our own written ones.

One of those laws, which we carry deep inside us, is intuition. It is lodged in a place that even the grave-robbing doctors could not discover. It's a blood-written code that directs us through life. The founder of this healing center, Sigrid Ueblacker, depends on this inner knowing. She watches, listens, and feels her way to an understanding of each eagle and owl. This vision, as I call it, directs her own daily work at healing the injured birds and returning them to the wild.

"Sweep the snow away," she tells me. "The Swainsons' hawks should be in Argentina this time of year and should not have to stand in the snow."

I sweep.

And that is in the winter when the hands ache from the cold, and the water freezes solid and has to be broken out for the birds, fresh buckets carried over icy earth from the well. In summer, it's another story. After only a few hours the food begins to move again, as if resurrected to life. A rabbit shifts a bit. A mouse turns. You could say that they have been resurrected, only with a life other than the one that left it. The moving skin swarms with flies and their offspring, ants, and a few wasps, busy at their own daily labor.

Even aside from the expected rewards for this work, such as seeing an eagle healed and winging across the sky it fell from, there are others. An occasional snake, beautiful and sleek, finds its way into the cage one day, eats a mouse and is too fat to leave, so we watch its long muscular life stretched out in the tall grasses. Or, another summer day, taking branches to be burned with a pile of wood near the little creek, a large turtle with a dark and shining shell slips soundlessly into the water, its presence a reminder of all the lives beyond these that occupy us.

One green morning, an orphaned owl perches nervously above me while I clean. Its downy feathers are roughed out. It appears to be twice its size as it clacks its beak at me, warning me to stay back. Then, fearing me the way we want it to, it bolts off the perch and flies, landing by accident on the wooden end of my rake, before it sees that a human is an extension of the tool, and it flies again to a safer place while I return to raking.

The word *rake* means to gather or heap up, to smooth the broken ground. That's what this work is, all of it, the smoothing over of broken ground, the healing of the severed trust we humans hold with earth. We gather it back together again with great care, take the broken pieces and fragments and return them to the sky. It is work at the borderland between species, at the boundary between injury and healing.

There is an art to raking, a very fine art, one with rhythm in it, and life. On the days I do it well, the rake wakes up. Wood that came from dark dense forests seems to return to life. The water that rose up through the rings of that wood, the minerals of earth mined upward by the burrowing tree roots, all come alive. My own fragile hand touches the wood, a hand full of my own life, including that which rose each morning early to watch the sun return from the other side of the planet. Over time, these hands will smooth the rake's wooden handle down to a sheen.

Raking. It is a labor round and complete, smooth and new as an egg, and the rounding seasons of the world revolving in time and space. All things, even our own heartbeats and sweat, are in it, part of it.

And that work, that watching the turning over of life, becomes a road into what is essential. Work is the country of hands, and they want to live there in the dailiness of it, the repitition that is time's language of prayer, a common tongue. Everything is there, in that language, in the humblest of labor. The rake wakes up and the healing is in it. The shadows of leaves that once fell beneath the tree the handle came from are in that labor, and the rabbits that passed this way, on the altar of our work. And when the rake wakes up, all earth's gods are reborn, and they dance and sing in the dusty air around us.

WALKING

IT BEGAN IN DARK AND UNDERGROUND WEATHER, A slow hunger moving toward light. It grew in a dry gulley beside the road where I live, a place where entire hillsides are sometimes yellow, windblown tides of sunflower plants. But this plant was different. It was alone and larger than the countless others that had established their lives farther up the hill. This one was a traveler, a settler, and like a dream beginning in conflict, it grew where the land had been disturbed.

I saw it first in early summer. It was a green and sleeping bud, raising itself toward the sun. Ants worked around the unopened bloom, gathering aphids and sap. A few days later, it was a tender young flower, soft and new, with a pale green center and a troop of silver-gray insects climbing up and down the stalk. Over the summer this sunflower grew into a plant of incredible beauty, turning its face daily toward the sun in the most subtle of ways, the black center of it dark and alive with a deep blue light, as if flint had sparked an elemental fire there, in community with rain, mineral, mountain air, and sand.

As summer changed from green to yellow there were new visitors daily, the lace-winged insects, the bees whose legs were fat with pollen, and grasshoppers with their clattering wings and desperate hunger. There were other lives I missed, those too small or hidden to see. It was as if this plant with its host of lives was a society, one in which moment by moment, depending on light and moisture, there was great and diverse change.

There were changes in the next larger world around the plant as well. One day I rounded a bend in the road to find the disturbing sight of a dead horse, black and still against a hillside, eyes rolled back. Another day I was nearly lifted by a wind and sandstorm so fierce and hot that I had to wait for it to pass before I could return home. On this day the faded dry petals of the sunflower were swept across the land. That was when the birds arrived to carry the new seeds to another future.

In this one plant, in one summer season, a drama of need and survival took place. Hungers were filled.

Insects coupled. There was escape, exhaustion, and
death. Lives touched down a moment and were gone.

I was an outsider. I only watched. I never learned
the sunflower's golden language or the tongues of its
citizens. I had a small understanding, nothing more
than a shallow observation of the flower, insects, and
birds. But they knew what to do, how to live. An old
voice from somewhere, gene or cell, told the plant
how to evade the pull of gravity and find its way
upward, how to open. It was instinct, intuition, necessity. A certain knowing directed the seed-bearing
birds on paths to ancestral homelands they had never
seen. They believed it. They followed.

There are other summons and calls, some even
more mysterious than those commandments to birds
or those survival journeys of insects. In bamboo
plants, for instance, with their thin green canopy of
light and golden stalks that creak in the wind. Once a
century, all of a certain kind of bamboo flower on the
same day. Neither the plants' location, in Malaysia or
in a greenhouse in Minnesota, nor their age or size
make a difference. They flower. Some current of an
inner language passes among them, through space
and separation, in ways we cannot explain in our language. They are all, somehow, one plant, each with a
share of communal knowledge.

John Hay, in *The Immortal Wilderness*, has written: "There are occasions when you can hear the
mysterious language of the Earth, in water, or coming through the trees, emanating from the mosses,
seeping through the undercurrents of the soil, but
you have to be willing to wait and receive."

Sometimes I hear it talking. The light of the sunflower was one language, but there are others more audible. Once, in the redwood forest, I heard a beat, something like a drum or heart coming from the ground and trees and wind. That underground current stirred a kind of knowing inside me, a kinship and longing, a dream barely remembered that disappeared back to the body. Another time, there was the booming voice of an ocean storm thundering from far out at sea, telling about what lived in the distance, about the rough water that would arrive, wave after wave revealing the disturbance at center.

Tonight I walk. I am watching the sky. I think of the people who came before me and how they knew the placement of stars in the sky, watched the moving sun long and hard enough to witness how a certain angle of light touched a stone only once a year. Without written records, they knew the gods of every night, the small, fine details of the world around them and of immensity above them.

Walking, I can almost hear the redwoods beating. And the oceans are above me here, rolling clouds, heavy and dark, considering snow. On the dry, red road, I pass the place of the sunflower, that dark and secret location where creation took place. I wonder if it will return this summer, if it will multiply and move up to the other stand of flowers in a territorial struggle.

It's winter and there is smoke from the fires. The square, lighted windows of houses are fogging over. It is a world of elemental attention, of all things working together, listening to what speaks in the

blood. Whichever road I follow, I walk in the land of
many gods, and they love and eat one another. Walking, I am listening to a deeper way. Suddenly all my
ancestors are behind me. Be still, they say. Watch and
listen. You are the result of the love of thousands.